African Poetry and the English Language

John Haynes

MACMILLAN
PUBLISHERS

© John Haynes, 1987

First published 1987

Published by *Macmillan Publishers Ltd*
London and Basingstoke
Associated companies and representatives in Accra,
Auckland, Delhi, Dublin, Gaborone, Hamburg, Harare,
Hong Kong, Kuala Lumpur, Lagos, Manzini, Melbourne,
Mexico City, Nairobi, New York, Singapore, Tokyo

Printed in Hong Kong

British Library Cataloguing in Publication Data
Haynes, John
    African poetry and the English language.
    1. African poetry (English) — History and
    criticism
    I. Title
    821   PR9342

ISBN 0-333-44928-2

To comrades in Drama Village, Zaria (1980-86):
Oga Abah, Awam Amkpa, Salihu Bappa, Brian Crow,
Michael Etherton, Rachel Ewu, Egwugwu Illah,
Mbulelo Mzamane, Jenks Okwori

Acknowledgements

Some of these essays appeared first in slightly different versions in the journals *Ariel, Journal of Commonwealth Literature, Saiwa, Research in African Literatures*, and one as part of an Ife Monograph on Literature and Criticism. Acknowledgements are due to the editors of these publications.

The author and publishers wish to thank the following who have kindly given permission for the use of copyright material:

Jonathan Cape Ltd on behalf of the Estate of Pablo Neruda for an extract from 'I Will Come Back', translated by Alastair Reid, from *Selected Poems*, edited by Nathaniel Tarn;

Rex Collings Ltd for 'In Search of Roots' by S. Sipamla from *The Soweto I Love* (1977);

Ad Donker (Pty) Ltd for 'Throb V' and 'The Actual Dialogue' from *Selected Poems* by Mangane Serote (1982);

East African Publishing House Limited on behalf of the Estate of the late Okot p'Bitek for an extract from *Song of Lawino, Song of Ocol* (1984);

Heinemann Educational Books Ltd for 'Distances' and 'Siren Limits IV' from *Labyrinths with Path of Thunder* by Christopher Okigbo; 'African Mfiti Flight No. 1' from *Summer Fires: New Poetry from Africa* (ed. Calder, Mapanje & Pietersen); extract from 'Emperor Shaka the Great by M. Kunene from *Emperor Shaka the Great* (1979); and Heinemann Kenya Ltd for an extract from 'I Will Marry when I Want' (1980) by Ngugi Wa Thiong'o and Ngugi wa Maririi;

Index on Censorship for an extract from 'It's no use' by Victor Jacinto Flecha (translator, Nick Caistor) from *Index on Censorship* Vol. 8, No. 1, p. 31;

Methuen London (by permission with Suhrkamp Verlag) for lines from *Poems, 1913–1956* by Bertolt Brecht (first English translation 1976);

Harold Ober Associates Inc for 'Dirge'; extracts from 'Songs of Sorrow' from *Modern Poetry from Africa* (Editors U Beier and G Moore) (1968) and 'Five' from *Guardians of the Sacred* (1974) by Dr Kofi Awoonor;

Penguin Books Ltd for an extract from 'Great and Strong' from Selected Poems by Miroslav Holub (translated by Ian Milner and George Theiner) (Penguin Modern European Poets, 1967);

Stand Magazine for an extract from 'Travel Tickets' by Samih-al-Qasim from *Stand Magazine*, Vol. 22, No. 1 (Newcastle).

Contents

Preface

These essays were written at different times, but they form a unity of interest and approach. This is non-linear; different themes and topics occur throughout the overall pattern, the same ideas being approached from different directions, different essays emphasising one or another facet of the whole. They can be read in any order.

In composing an introductory essay with the collection as a whole in mind an attempt has been made to illuminate the broad conception of poetry assumed in the essays. Each is, however, self-explanatory and the reader who is not interested in theory may prefer to skip the introductory study of poety in relation to ordinary conversation.

The approach to African poetry taken in the book is *through* the insights of linguistics, but relatively little space has been given to linguistics as such. The advocacy is certainly towards greater attention to the linguistic medium, since poetry as an art demands that, and also, since there has been hardly any close commentary on individual African poems, connecting interpretation to the details of language.

The commentaries are also intended to throw some light on a number of current issues in the practice and study of African poetry. These have been raised in a controversial way, which I mainly mistrust, but to which I am indebted in *Towards the Decolonization of African Literature*. Other issues, particularly the issue of English as a viable literary language for African literature, derive from the writings of Ngugi wa Thiong'O, and the work of Michael Etherton and the Drama Village at Ahmadu Bello University, Nigeria.

There are some issues which have been raised on my own account: the relation between orality and literacy in poetry, the linguistic signification of ideology and the subject, and the relations between poems and other kinds of text.

CHAPTER 1

Poetry and Conversation

Conversation is the discourse in which everyone participates. Even the deaf and dumb person knows a role in it. Before a baby has learnt how to speak, it is cast as a listener, and in that role learns how to speak, developing the part like an actor who identifies with and 'becomes' a character, the part which in a general form society has scripted for it as a 'subject'[1], that of a boy, a girl, the son of a beggar, the daughter of an emir. The first sounds from the cot, not yet words, have the rise and fall of conversational intonation, the contours of which the 'utterer' will probably remain largely unaware until he or she encounters a foreign language, or poetry. In conversations all the fundamental lessons are learnt, and although some deal with people and things which are not present to the speakers, most are intermeshed with practical experience, where talking, thinking, and doing are of a piece. And although words are distinct from things and people, ultimately, whatever material or other reality the world may have, it is as complexes of meanings, or 'texts', that it impinges on a person, and these are embedded in the categories of language, categories which, in turn, events and experience modify.

The to-and-fro of conversation, and its commonness and apparent lack of ritual, set it apart from poetry, which is usually a one-way communication, self-conscious, and in modern times, carefully composed in writing before being performed. Yet, despite these striking differences, poetry and other verbal arts, can in a sense be 'derived' from conversation. The linguistic resources used by both are the same, and conversations often contain poetry. A distinction must be made between *poetry* as a way of using language, which may occur in texts of almost all types, and *poems* which are whole texts specially devoted to that way of using language.

In the course of a conversation someone may say,

I went to the office again and again and again!

Here the repeated mention of the word 'again' mimes the repeated journeys the speaker has had to make. Not only do the grammar and intonation reinforce the meaning, but the act of utterance itself is highlighted, and textuality as such is displayed, as it is when the classmates of a girl with the name of Omotayo tease her by asking if she 'washes whiter'. Or, in discussing a doubtful deal with his lawyer, the businessman may fix the former with a meaningful gaze and say,

I have parked my car in the rain

and by the tone of voice and the gaze the lawyer will know that the man is not talking literally about his car, but about the fact that he has exposed himself to the legal 'weather', and is thus hinting that he will give him a handsome fee if he can fix the case. The example is like a proverb in which a form of words representing a particular situation is uttered so that the listener can savour it, and look *into* the text. Poetry, as it is being described here, is a way of using language so that the hearer is aware of *how* the speaker utters *as* he utters. Its object may be a mere play upon a name, or a description, or a 'gesture' towards an unstated innuendo or 'theme'.

A curious listener may, of course, interpret something in a poetic way, which is not intended as such, an unrealised pun, or a revealing assocation of words. One speaker is discussing a film seen the previous evening on the television, and mentions that it was immoral. Then the listener changes, or appears to change, the subject and asks how the speaker's wife is. Perhaps because he is sensitive on the issue and suspects his wife of being unfaithful to him, the first speaker notices this transition, which could have been quite innocent. Again, the listener might be struck by the remark because the word 'immoral' was being used in a way he would not use it, and revealed the ideological world in which the speaker lived. Seeing the poetry in a text of whatever kind, is, then, a matter of looking behind the scenes to see how it has been produced, linguistically speaking, which options in the linguistic system the speaker has chosen to use, and which he has avoided in the course of 'realising' his meaning in the grammar, and the sounds of language[2]. Like advertisements, poems appeal to the emotions and contain implicit or explicit propaganda. But the difference between the two is that the advertiser on the whole hopes that the reader or viewer will not look too closely into his text to see how he is being manipulated, while the poet hopes that he will look closely and see not so much what he, the poet, is saying, as what he has discovered in language. Imagine a person quoting an advertisement with the aim of revealing its sleight of hand. Now it is being held up ironically (or bitterly) for examination as poetic language.

The bitterness or irony are aspects of what the speaker means by his utterance, and of his act in mocking, displaying, criticising. The emotional impact of the remark derives from its relation to action, to the role the person has, not just as the speaker of this remark, but in wider life, and the role in which he is identified and identifies himself.

A poem – that is, a text devoted to the poetic use of language – can be 'derived' from conversation in the sense that it resembles a long conversational turn. This was the way in which Bertolt Brecht described drama. He thought of drama as an extension of the way in which a man describes how he saw an accident[3]. He speaks, uses gestures, acts out the expression and posture of the shocked driver, and so on. A play is a whole text, devoted to this. The derivation of the poem from the conversational turn is materialist in outlook in that each aspect of the poetic 'code' (or set of conventions as to what to listen for when we know we are hearing a poem) is related to a practical problem of communication. This follows Brecht's view of drama, and the ideas of Labov and Pratt[4] on 'natural narrative'.

In a real conversation each turn slots in with the one before and prepares the way for the one to follow. But when one speaker has a story to relate, like the man describing the accident, he can expect the other speakers to keep quiet, so long as he can command their interest. He hopes that by the time he has finished they will be better informed about the accident, and expects the turns after his narration to fill it out by discussion. Perhaps he is able to direct their thoughts not just to what actually happened, which driver was wrong, but to wider issues, the suffering that comes to innocent people when driving licences can be bought, whether it is a result of natural human weakness, or not. In this way he may hope to achieve a change in attitudes, and get people to complain. Not everyone could sustain a long turn of this kind. To do so demands a skill with words, and what keeps his listeners' attention is, in part, their enjoyment of his performance. In the oral tradition in Africa the institutionalised story-telling, or poetry performance, does not wait for a particular event such as an accident to happen. But still the conversation-like interaction is maintained. The poet and his audience are face-to-face, unlike the modern writer-poet and his readers, and they can comment as he goes along, or even intervene with questions, corrections or an alternative version. And in this context, more attention is given to the audience's role in evaluating the performance, by not going away, giving money, clapping, and so on, than it would be in the spontaneous conversation about an accident. But still, in most African traditions, the didactic thread is prominent. The poet is, in one sense or another, a teacher. The poet now has to actively look for material to sing about, not wait for accidents which he may happen to witness, and he has an obligation to his village or group to say something that is interesting and morally important, and to do it skilfully, and usually also in the way in which they have come to expect poets to perform.

The techniques of poetry can also be derived from the situation. The oral poet needs to compose 'on his feet', or to recall long poems he or someone else has previously composed. A metre and a rhyme scheme help with this, as does supporting music to which these are matched, and striking turns of phrase. Frequent repetition, and parallelism give him time to think, and ensure that the audience will hear everything. The same features help the audience to keep the text in their minds, repeat it to themselves, and so mull over it long after the preformance, and perhaps sing it to someone else. In origin, then, these technical features are practical. They are retained, however, after the text has ceased to depend on them for survival. They become distinguishing marks of the genre, part of the 'way poetry is composed'.

Hence written poetry still retains traces of its oral form, and the music which was the basis of its metrical rhythms. In written form it does not have to be memorised, but it may still be memorable, and require the same verbal skills in managing the metres. These now aid the poet in composition in a different way, by providing an objective framework which limits his options and forces him to be linguistically resourceful. Written poetry can be performed, but often it is not, and then it has no ritual or defining context beyond the published and printed book. But the code of reading is still oral, and since it is separated from the still and silent print, the inexperienced reader may be at a loss as to how to take a poem, what sort of communication it should manifest.

Since the written page preserves the written part of the text, some poets no longer use the stylistic features derived from performance and music. In modern African poetry in English most poets compose free verse. It is set out in lines on the page, may contain original turns of phrase, and be rhythmical in a non-metrical way, but now it is much like ordinary conversation, especially if the poet aims for a simple, accessible style. Then the status of the text as a poem depends almost entirely on how it is approached by a reader, whether or not he looks *into* the text.

The problem arises here as to whether, now, a poem is different from an ordinary conversational turn of the same length and can be interpreted on its own. Some poets have highlighted this question by presenting 'found poems', which are texts copied out from adver-tisements, diaries, or other sources, and presented out of the original context, as poems. Now by transposing them from the setting where they were functional, to the page where they are to be looked into, they become striking as samples of textuality. All poetry depends on the capacity of linguistic structures to operate in different, often contrasting, texts and contexts – what was traditionally called 'allusion', and now, looked at in different ways, is called 'intertextuality'.

Yet the blurring of the distinction between poems and other kinds of text has raised severe theoretical problems. At the same time it has put the reader into a strikingly active role, even while he remains silent, since now his contribution to the text by taking it as a poem, sometimes without any stylistic cues from the poet, restores him to a position analogous to the audience in an oral performance. The intervention of the reader of this unmarked kind of poem has become crucial, and the found poem is actually created by the reader's response.

Most actual African poems are by no means unmarked: they do reveal the deliberate craft of the poet. Because the poet is separated from his reader, however, the latter can never be certain what the poet 'put there'. Yet, if the model of conversation is retained (and many theoreticians would not retain it) an assumption is made by the reader that the poet did mean something by writing his poem, and part of that meaning is the offering of the text to the reader to explore, a sharing of what is in the language, and by extension in the culture. Of course the reader acts on faith and communicates with a reader he must imagine and may very well misconceive. But an imaginative identification of this kind is not peculiar to poetry; it is how we perceive and communicate under all circumstances, in the sense that all interaction depends upon our imaginary pictures of other people, whether they are physically before us or not.

One function of conversation in early childhood is the development of an imaginary role with which the child identifies, and through which he or she is identified. Indeed, what has been called 'interest' or emotional involvement, and in literature, commitment, is primarily a matter of imaginary identification with a text. To look at how it was produced linguistically is to look at it in the projected role of the writer, who in turn projected himself into the role of reader when writing. He must do so since a writer has to decide what a reader needs to know to make sense of the text in the scripting of which he has no role – except as imagined in this way. The ghostly interaction mimes the way in which the individual subject is *produced* in a complex of interpenetrating texts[5].

A writer must weave his text so as to take account of the questions and objections which would have been expressed in conversation, or to some extent in an oral performance. Some of these questions will deliberately not be met, and the reader will be provoked strategically to look closely into his text, there being no other way to gain 'clarification'.

Questioning the status of the author, and the phenomenon of the 'found' poem remind us that the poet manipulates and presents texts composed of a language he did not create. He 'finds' it, as the poet who transposes an advertisement to his notebook does, and as the child finds his name and a mapped-out role. The poet quotes the grammar and phonology of his language, and other texts in it, so that we notice them. The language of poetry is itself usually designed to be quotable. When the reader or performer utters the text he quotes it.

What he means by these allusions and quotations, and by the vocabulary of English, is not completely under his control, and the reader, looking into his poem, may find in it meanings which the poet has conveyed in spite of himself, as someone may 'betray' his thoughts, or feelings. The reader interprets not just the poem but also the poet. Paradoxically the poet is treated like a child or a madman who does not know his own mind. And indeed, in some cultures, poets have been compared to inspired madmen or thought to have the insight of children. Yet in these same societies it may be believed that no one really knows his own mind except the sage.

A reader takes an active role when he writes a text which is analogous to a conversational reply to the poet's turn. This is the position from which the essays in this book are written. They are replies in the sense that, for the most part, they attempt to articulate the process of reading, the tacit conversational moves prompted by different texts. Most are close commentaries on the journey through the texts. This process of looking into poems (or other texts) is not finally distinguishable from looking into their ideological underpinnings. This convergence has led some theorists to see an identity of interest between poetry and political understanding, and to urge that the proper study of linguistics is poetry, since poetry makes the most fundamental workings of language the object of attention[6].

The text of a poem is most stable and objective at the levels of substance (print) and form (grammar and vocabulary). At the level of discourse (meaning), the ideational (referential) component is relatively stable when the text is literal and refers to an immediate material setting. The wider ideational force is less stable, however, since the theme of a modern poem normally has to be extrapolated by a reader or hearer, and that person's view of life may influence how he or she does this. Least stable is the interpersonal component of the discourse, the emotional significance and immediacy the poem may have for its audience.

The emotional impact of a poem, or 'interest' as it may be called, does relate the poet (however imaginatively) to his reader in terms of intimacy or solidarity, but may vary a great deal from reader to reader, listener to listener. It is difficult to express in conventional western literary criticism, which tends to neglect it in favour of ideational features; but it is most clearly expressed in performance, which is always also intepretation. In performance a good deal of the indeterminacy of the printed poem, or script, can be removed.

The interest a reader or listener has in a poem is a matter of its relation beyond the theatre, or café, or classroom in which he experiences it, to his everyday life, his social praxis; also it depends upon his capacity to make and sustain such a relation. It is here, in the reader's practical response, that commitment should be considered. A poem will call up different related texts, or 'connotations' in different readers, and in Africa these may be in a variety of languages. The poem may be immediately related to a social crisis for some readers or classes of reader, and much more remotely so related for others. A poem by a Soweto poet such as Serote, about Soweto, has more immediate interest to a Soweto schoolchild, than to a Nigerian lecturer. What may be obvious to one may be 'obscure' to another for this reason, and require academic footnotes. Interest, in the sense in which it is used above has been insufficiently studied. Yet in African literature it is widely assumed that poems are composed to be performed, which implies an imaginative contribution by the performer, and by his audience. Each performance of a poem takes place under specific circumstances, and these may make it dramatically different on different occasions. Consider the following poem by Mongane Serote, written in the Soweto context.

THROB V

My heart has been cut between sharp scissors
why because my life depends on stealing
and my conscience has been screaming
because I lie too much for survival[7]

The interest of the Soweto schoolchild in this poem would be connected with powerlessness, how the 'stealing', partly literal though it might be, is also cultural, how the black has been forced to steal his own culture from white domination. When he 'lies' it is to deny his culture for the sake of work-permit or job. Suppose this text were transferred to the lips of the dubious businessman in conversation with his lawyer. Now the 'stealing' becomes the popular Nigerian conception of 'looting' and other kinds of 'business' among the new middle class, and yet the 'lie' of denying his own people by alliance, however hypocritical, with western interests, still threatens his ultimate survival. The businessman himself may well not see this, and certainly would not desire to, but a Nigerian performer in his role, and a Nigerian audience, very possibly would. But clearly the angles from which they and the Sowetan approach this denial and threat are different. Yet in another, ideational sense, and in its print and wording, the poem is 'the same' in both contexts.

The academic type of literary criticism which informs modern African education systems tends to de-emphasise interest, though it has been given more importance in recent post-structuralist and semiotic approaches to literature. Academic literary criticism tends to put forward a canonical interpretation of the text of a poem from the viewpoint of the poet and his cultural and other contexts. 'Commentary', such as is attempted in the essays in this book, is less restricted, and aims partly to do this, but more centrally to retrace the experience of reading and responding to the text. A commentary aims to reproduce the way in which the reader, in his context, traces the linguistic twists and turns of the poet's text, experienced as a process which develops through time (the textual function of language)[8], and which he elaborates into wider thematic significances (the ideational function), and which he connects to his own praxis, his interest (interpersonal function). Commentary is not primarily judgement or assessment. The approval is embodied in the commentator's thinking it worth writing the commentary, and as a reader in his capacity to sustain his interest in the text. Disapproval is also practical, and expressed by the reader's not wanting to finish reading the poem, or not wanting to read it again. The value of the poem, and whether the reader thinks it really amounts to a poem, follow from the attempt to read it as one.

The aim of commentary may simply be to make explicit and articulate a particular reader's response, so that it may be shared, as enthusiasm or admiration may be shared. It may also be proferred as a contribution to the development of poetic techniques, by revealing how particular poems work at the level of craft. The development of African poetry is in the hands, not of critics or commentators, but of the poets themselves; and the best contribution the commentator can make is in the practical domain of composition.

If the commentator is to trace the strands and threads of the poet's thought, and then to make this tracing articulate (as many readers will not, but still understand and respond to the text), then he needs to have a further discourse in which to do this. In the following essays this has been drawn from systemic linguistics, which forms a coherent description of English, and provides a means of relating the details of form and substance to wider contextual and ideological features of poetry. If the commentator, and the commentator's reader, are to come into contact with the texts of poems as poems – and not as prose paraphrases – this approach through language is essential. Poetry is a verbal art. To be involved in it is to be involved with language as such, as an object of wonder and as something that lies in the depths of ourselves as human beings, and as subjects. And it is only through some knowledge of how language works, as a whole, that the full fascination and 'magic' of a poet's thought can be experienced.

The movement of literary and related studies towards the study of language and the semiotics of the text in recent years has led to fundamental questioning of conceptions of life which have been central to western culture and to the conceptions of education it has exported to African countries, in particular the idea of the self-contained individual subject, and in literature of the criteria for counting this or that text as a poem or a novel or indeed 'literary' in any special sense at all. This approach, adapted and perhaps distorted as it is in this and other essays in this book, can certainly help to *show* something about African poetry in English, if in the end it cannot fully *say* enough. It is hoped that the necessary centricity of this point of view, and of the author, is sufficiently explicit for the reader to make his or her own readings of the poems clearer to him or herself.

The main emphasis in the essays is on the relation between discourse and form, on 'close reading' in the context of a wider democratic Marxist interpretation of contemporary Africa, in particular of Nigeria, and on the notion of performance in discussions of texts. This runs counter to much traditional literary criticism, and stylistic analysis, and also to prominent aspects of the post-structuralist school just alluded to. But it reflects a traditional feature of African poetry as a discourse which is never clearly separable from drama. This is the direction of, the 'logic of' the book, and the dimension of African poetic discourse that requires further study[9].

NOTES

1 The term 'subject' and others used in technical or semi-techical senses are explained in the Glossary. This is arranged in alphabetical order.

2 See Glossary. Also M.A.K. Halliday, 'Modes of Meaning and Modes of Expression: types of grammatical structure and their determination by different semantic functions', D.J. Allerton, Edward Carney and David Holdcroft (eds), *Function and Context in Linguistic Analysis: Essays Offered to William Haas* (Cambridge: Cambridge University Press, 1979) pp. 57, 79. Halliday uses the term 'semantics' in a way in which it has become more common recently to use the term 'discourse'. See under 'Semantics' in the Glossary.

3 See John Willet (ed.) *Brecht on Theatre: The Development of an Aesthetic* (London: Eyre Methuen, 1974), p. 212ff.

4 See Mary Louise Pratt, *Towards a Speech Act Theory of Literary Discourse* (Bloomington: Indiana University Press, 1977)

5 See Glossary on 'Intertextuality'.

6 Julia Kristeva, *Desire in Language: A Semiotic Approach to Literature and Art* (Oxford: Basil Blackwell, 1980), p. 25.

7 Mongane Wally Serote, 'Anonymous Throbs + a Dream' in *Selected Poems*, Johannesburg: Ad Donker (1982), p. 70.

8 See note 2 above.

9 I am indebted to the example of colleagues in Drama Village at Ahmadu Bello University, Zaria, Nigeria, for inspiration in this direction.

CHAPTER 2

Discourse and Form in Soyinka's 'Post Mortem'[1] and 'Dawn'[2]

Most of this essay is devoted to 'Post Mortem'; the discussion of 'Dawn' is introduced to develop some points made about 'Post Mortem'. The tendency among some commentators to disparage Soyinka's work, especially his poetry, in very general terms, because of its alleged 'obscurity', 'elitism', 'irrelevance' or 'eurocentricity' by both populists[3] and Marxists,[4] may obscure the great interest of his techniques as a poet. Even those who accept his limitations as a poet, and who find his culturalism unsympathetic, cannot afford simply to dismiss his poetry out of hand. There is much to be learned from it. What follows, then, is focused on the positive contributions these poems, as examples, make to the technique of African poetry in English, which other poets need to bear in mind, and perhaps develop.

The interest of 'Post Mortem' is the way the linguistic medium is highlighted at the level of discourse, that is, at the level of the roles reader and poet (as the reader imagines him) play. 'Dawn', by contrast, highlights linguisticity[5] at the level of grammatical form and vocabulary.

Language is stratified. It consists of three broad levels which can be summarised as follows.

DISCOURSE: the level of meanings, subdivided into layers: ideational, interpersonal, textual[6]

FORM: the level of grammatical structure and vocabulary.

SUBSTANCE: the level of meaningful sound (phonology) or written signs (graphology)

The levels are related to each other as a sign and its interpretation are related to each other, as a code. But there is no one-to-one correlation between units at one level and units at another. The same sentence can have different meanings in different circumstances. 'Post Mortem' exploits this lack of close correlation between the levels of discourse and form: the same words may be given different, indeed contrastive, sense depending on whether they are looked at from a typical western viewpoint or from a typical Yoruba one.

Poetry has certain conventions[7] which govern, or at least influence, the way in which the reader, and the poet as he anticipates his effect on the reader, looks at the text. The reader looks *into* the text, takes note of apparently trivial details, seeks a philosophical theme, a personal and emotional significance, and a cumulative development in the text. In much modern poetry attention to linguisticity tends to concentrate at the level of discourse. Unlike the typical traditional poem there is less highlighting of phonology, in the use of rhymes and metres, and often no attempt to draw attention to structure by startling juxtaposition of words. The feature of 'Post Mortem' to be studied here is its linguisticity at the level of discourse.

POST MORTEM

There are more functions to a freezing plant	1
than stocking beer; cold biers of mortuaries	2
submit their dues, harnessed – glory be! –	3
is the cold hand of death . . .	4
his mouth was cotton filled, his man-pike	5
shrunk to sub-soil grub	6
his head was hollowed and his brain	7
on scales – was this a trick to prove	8
fore-knowledge after death?	9
his flesh confesses what has stilled	10
his tongue; masked fingers think from him	11
to learn, how not to die.	12
let us love all things of grey; grey slabs	13
grey scalpel, one grey sleep and form,	14
grey images.	15

The poem represents an immediate situation in which a surgeon is performing a post-mortem. The freezing plant, the scalpel, and so on, indicate a modern hospital and the practice of a scientific method of finding out the cause of death. This situation *in* the poem (the 'imaginary situation') can be contrasted with the situation *of* the poem, that is the relation between the text and its reader and composer, and how the text fits into the preconceptions of this or that reader's commonsense world. It may be assumed, as elsewhere in Soyinka's work, that the reader he envisages is familiar with and sympathetic to a traditional Yoruba cosmology. In what follows the shorthand term 'Yoruba reader' will be used for this envisaged reader. This reader will be contrasted to the assumed 'western' scientific cosmology of the surgeon. He forms part of the 'imaginary situation', while the Yoruba reader forms part of the 'practical situation'. The richness of the poem derives from the way the poet refers to an imaginary situation in which western scientific values of detachment are assumed, but continually makes gestures towards the Yoruba reader whose ideology is quite different. The discrepancy has the effect of undermining and mocking what to the Yoruba reader appear the narrow scientific preoccupations of the practical situation.

In the first line of the poem the gesture to the Yoruba reader is clearcut enough:

There are more functions to a freezing plant
than stocking beer

In other words, 'although you may associate freezers with stocking beer, in this situation these people use a freezer for storing a corpse'. By bringing the idea of beer into juxtaposition with corpses Soyinka draws an implicit comparison between the convivial situation of parties and enjoyment, and that of death. The tone of voice suggested to a performer of the poem is one of casual joking, and so is callous. The ironic flippancy suggests that what the surgeon is doing is also essentially flippant and unfeeling. He assumes a different attitude to death in the reader. And this view is more nearly made explicit at the end of the poem where he adopts a tone of solidarity, addressing his reader now directly for the first time coupled with himself, as 'us', and appealing to the sense of love:

let us love all things of grey...

In a written poem the tone of voice can only be suggested. In performance it realises the 'tenor' of discourse. The expected tenor in the presence of a dead body is different from the expected tenor before a fridge full of beer. But Soyinka mixes them up. He goes on,

...cold biers of mortuaries
submit their dues...

The flippant pun on 'beers' and 'biers' is completely irreverent, and so is the personification (of a corpse's resting place) in the expression 'submit their dues'. This phrase is usually employed in standard English in the social situation of paying a subscription, or perhaps rent or rates, at regular intervals and as an accepted part of routine bourgeois life. The placing of this expression here is, in effect, a quotation from a typical non-poetic text, for example a notice in a social club that all members should 'submit their dues' by a certain date. In Soyinka's clause the submitter of the dues is 'cold biers', as if the frozen slabs were submitting not cash or cheques, but dead bodies as their own kind of routine payment. This idea is likely to suggest a different type of text to the Yoruba reader; it recalls the god Ogun who exacts his own 'dues' which are indeed often in the form of corpses, as sacrifices. The difference between paying your life to the god and paying your yearly subscription to the club secretary carries with it a difference of tenor and of cosmology.

The next comment in the poem is interrupted by the exclamation, 'glory be!' which might well be a quotation from a religious text, itself an interruption in the church service by the enthusiastic worshipper. The interruption in the poem mimes the typical role of the expression as an interruption in a service. But the surrounding text in the poem is not of the type which would provoke this enthusiastic contribution. Soyinka's insertion of it seems again to be ironical and flippant, bringing the western religious text into an imaginary situation where what is going on is not a service but a different kind of ritual, the coldly detached analysis of the parts of a corpse. The coldness is attested to in the clause interrupted:

harnessed. . .
is the cold hand of death. . .

This includes the well-worn cliché, 'the cold hand of death'. It takes on an added, again flippant, point when it is recalled that the hand in question in the morgue is not only cold but frozen as well, on a slab. Soyinka relies on his Yoruba reader's having a sufficiently close knowledge of standard English to recognise that the expression *is* a cliché. Death is 'harnessed' in a simple physical sense by being held in icy suspension; but 'harnessed' may also mean 'controlled' in the sense that the surgeon can explain the mystery of death by a scientific analysis, by using his gloves, his scalpel, and his scales. But death, as the last stanza of the poem suggests and as traditional Yoruba cosmology holds, is not so simply encompassed and isolated – or, to use Soyinka's word, 'compartmentalised'[8] – as the western approach may suggest. Death cannot be analysed out of existence or profound significance, any more than it can be held in stillness by ice. In Yoruba cosmology, on the contrary, death, is omnipresent and contemporary with life, and its contemplation indicative of human seriousness. Both the naive convert to Christianity who cries 'glory be' and the surgeon at his slab trivialise death in their rituals. They try to 'harness' it by, in effect, not facing it.

As the poem moves on, the abstraction, death, becomes personified. The corpse is now 'he'.

> his mouth was cotton filled, his man-pike
> shrunk to sub-soil grub
>
> his head was hollowed and his brain
> on scales...

The body is being reduced to discrete parts, compartmentalised by dissection, and by the way in which the poet separates out the different parts, the mouth, the genitals, the brain, and before this, the hand. The brain being weighed on scales is a striking image of the western cerebral approach to life, as the Yoruba reader will see it. The brain and the body are *reduced* to what is measurable, and detached from the life of the impulses symbolised by the genitals. The metaphors used to describe the dead man's genitals may seem at first sight odd in that it is difficult to imagine how a steel pike can 'shrink' into an organic grub. Yet the 'man-pike' is a 'weapon' and hence destructive and so associated with death, while (as the penis) it is also creative and life-giving. A comparison to attributes of Ogun emerges. The transformation of the iron weapon into the organic grub is a metamorphosis from inanimate to animate, the reverse of the movement from animate body to inanimate corpse. This modifies the assumption, attributable to the surgeon, that death is not fertile, life not destructive, that the two are conceptually distinct and mutually exclusive. In traditional Yoruba cosmology death is not a linear end to life but coterminous with it. And this idea is taken up in the ensuing question,

> ...was this a trick to prove
> fore-knowledge after death?

A rhetorical question. In asking it the poet is encouraging the mockery of his Yoruba reader rather than seeking an answer. He deliberately mixes up the logic of time, the concepts of 'before' ('fore-knowledge') and 'after'. Logically, it is nonsensical to employ hindsight to predict the future, and hence the analytical method can be made to look futile, or at least negative, since the discoveries the surgeon may make obviously cannot predict anything or remedy anything. But the mixing-up of cause and effect by Soyinka may be seen as drawing attention to a different, Yoruba, perspective on time and linearity. In Yoruba thought the relation of life and death is not conceived in a 'before and after' manner, but rather cyclically[9]. A similar manipulation of the logic of death occurs in the next lines.

> his flesh confesses what has stilled
> his tongue; masked fingers think from him
> to learn, how not to die.

The 'stilled' tongue cannot speak up and tell the surgeon what the cause of death was. Probably the man never knew what was going on in his system anyway. But the flesh gives up its secrets when examined in the morgue, and in this sense is more informative than the man's voice would have been. Like a priest or a torturer, the surgeon wants to extort a confession, but it turns out to be something contradictory, 'how not to die'. Soyinka implies that the surgeon is motivated by a fear of death. From his own point of view the surgeon's quest is for ways of preventing other people dying from this or that illness prematurely, not to avoid death altogether. What the poet's phrasing suggests is that the dissection is an attempt to evade the meaning of mortality. A still closer ambiguity might be entertained. 'How to die', which allows the utterer to avoid mention of the grammatical subject of 'die', could be paraphrased as either: (a) He hopes to learn how he himself may avoid extinction; or: (b) He hopes to learn how the corpse does avoid extinction.
It is a difference between construing the clause as 'how not to die' and 'how to not die'. (b) assumes that death is not a final stage of entropy, while (a) assumes that it is. Both, to the traditional Yoruba, would be evasions.

The fingers of the surgeon are 'masked' in the transferred sense that the man wearing them is masked, also in the sense that he wears gloves, and further that they seal his hands and himself off from (Yoruba) reality. The attribution of thought and learning to the hands is another example of compartmentalisation of the human body. This atomised world is to be set against a different cosmology which lacks these clear-cut distinctions between life and death, the personal and the impersonal. And at the end of the poem the mention of 'love' brings this cosmology into the open. Love is a unifying and involving attitude to the very entities from which the post-mortem surgeon strives to detach himself. Grey is an indeterminate colour in which contrasts are neutralised, the colour also of the surgeon's blade and the dead man's brain, and of the brain's own synthesising images.

In this poem, then, Soyinka takes a modern imaginary situation and looks at it through the lens of a traditional cosmology. The reader is invited to play off a stylised scientific view against a stylised mythological one, which will find echoes in a number of traditional African cosmologies. An 'ideal' Yoruba reader has been assumed in this discussion; Soyinka seems to have in mind someone who is also aware of nuances in English discourses, and can pick up the quotations from different kinds of text in British usage. He quotes from these, and 'bounces them off' the Yoruba cosmology, setting up an interplay of contrastive interpretations of the same words and phrases from different viewpoints, much as French deconstructionist commentators do when they look at a text from a consciously exotic perspective, thus revealing the presuppositions which make up its composition.[10]

The picture of this poem as a text directed to this 'Yoruba' reader is, thus, an oversimplification. The actual reader stands 'behind' this reader, and registers his imagined responses. Otherwise the *interaction* between the two cosmologies would be impossible. Also, the comparison between Soyinka's strategy and deconstruction does not prevent the actual reader from looking at this strategy itself, and deconstructing that. Soyinka makes a distinction between the western mode of thought, which he characterises as 'compartmentalising'[11] and the African mode of thought which is 'accommodating'.[12] This cliché dies hard.[13] That Soyinka uses it is a measure of his confidence in the Yoruba cosmology to humanise technological life. The evocation of love in the last stanza of 'Post Mortem' suggests that the rituals of the surgeon with his blade can be subsumed under the Ogun cosmology in which death and life are integrated into a larger unity. But this way of thinking is also characteristic of European thought, particularly poetry, in the nineteenth century, and is typical of the reaction of artists to the growth of technological societies. Despite Soyinka's denials in his speech at the 1967 African-Scandinavian Writers' Conference,[14] it is difficult not to see in his questioning of compartmentalisation the expression of a dismay which African and European artists share, though it may be doubted whether traditional Yoruba religion can actually humanise modern Nigeria.

.Soyinka seems to take this European-versus-African polarity as the basis of his thinking about the post-mortem surgeon; but he admits that the positivistic attitude can be 'caught' by Africans. And a comment at the Scandinavian Writers' Conference suggests he has an African in mind in this poem, not an actual surgeon but an acculturated writer.

> When the writer in his own society can no longer function as a conscience, he must recognize that his choice lies between denying himself totally or withdrawing to the position of chronicler and post-mortem surgeon.[15]

There is, however, little in 'Post Mortem' which suggests a writer. The

thought comes to mind because I happen to have read both the poem and Soyinka's Stockholm speech. The point is mentioned, together with these doubts about the validity of the opposition between the African and the European in this ahistorical way, to draw attention to the wider encompassing role of the actual reader, who brings to the text various accidental experiences, and his own reservations about a poem.

Poetry is a form of discourse in which attention is directed to the linguistic medium itself, at all linguistic levels, including that of discourse, or interactive meanings. In 'Post Mortem', the double focus on the text is produced at the level of discourse. A particular stretch of text such as 'his head was hollowed' can be interpreted as either a straightforward factual report, or as a piece of mockery, depending on the speech act the reader holds in mind. The level of discourse is made up of three broad functions, the representational (ideational), the interactive (interpersonal) and the sequential (textual). What has been discussed so far is primarily inter-personal, that is, the speech act this or that stretch of language is to be interpreted as performing. It is from this, the interpersonal viewpoint, that the contrast between the two interpretations can be entertained. From the ideational point of view 'his head was hollowed' has the same meaning for any speaker, or reader. The poem does not make much use of poetic devices at the levels of form and substance.

If it does strike some readers as 'obscure' this may be because they fail to recognise the strategy of the poem, perhaps because they are unaware of the cosmology Soyinka presumes in his Yoruba, or otherwise sympa-thetic, reader. Such a reader may very well read and 'understand' all the sentences in this poem without understanding it as a poem, or how it is a poem. Thus the 'obscurity' and the poetry go together, as is typical of modernist writing.

To develop this point a little we may compare this poem briefly with 'Dawn', a more notoriously 'obscure' poem by Soyinka. This is the text.

DAWN

Breaking earth upon	1
A spring-haired elbow, lone	2
A palm beyond head-grains, spikes	3
A guard of prim fronds, piercing	4
high hairs of the wind	5
As one who bore the pollen highest	6
Blood-drops in the air, above	7
The even belt of tassels, above	8

Coarse leaf teasing on the waist, steals	9
The lone intruder, tearing wide	10
The chaste hide of the sky	11
O celebration of the rites of dawn	12
Night-spread in tatters and a god	13
Received, aflame with kernels.	14

In this poem attention is drawn to the medium at the level of form, that is, the choice of vocabulary and sentence structure. The reader is left in several minds about the interpretation, not so much of speech acts, as of words and syntax. Part of the initial difficulty a reader may have in discerning what the topic of the poem is comes from Soyinka's eschewal of the naturalistic mode of writing. He does not give us a direct description of a palm tree, the sun rising, and so on. The immediate situation we are to imagine is not marked out by direct reference to easily recognisable or typical features. In most texts the immediate situation, the scene the text is to evoke, is suggested by mention of a few telling details in the 'thesis' of the text, that is, what is actually mentioned in so many words. In describing a landscape it is impossible to mention everything; Soyinka selects 'breaking earth', 'a palm', 'the wind' and so on, but his selections are not sufficiently typical, or clichéd, to give his reader an immediate image of the scene. The problems of identifying what 'a springhaired elbow' is, or what the 'blood drops in the air' are, will be left unsolved in this account, which will be confined to the grammar.

The first long sentence spans the first eleven lines, and in it Soyinka seems to mime the idea of suspension. The development and inter-pretability of the sentences is held back by the rhetorical device of 'arrest'.[16] The expected resolution is delayed. For example, after the first clause,

Breaking earth upon
A spring-haired elbow . . .

the simplest resolution would be to move directly to the main clause, 'steals/The lone intruder' or, in a more typical sequence,

'Breaking earth upon a spring-haired elbow, the lone intruder steals (that is, into the landscape).'

But between the first clause, 'Breaking earth . . .' and the main one, Soyinka places a good deal of material which arrests this conclusion, just as the establishment of the sun's ascendancy in the sky, or of sexual consummation (suggested by the allusions to sexual texts in 'prim', 'teasing on the waist', 'chaste' and so on) are delayed in actual time. Also, just as in 'Post Mortem', the reader may entertain two perspectives on the discourse; here he may entertain two perspectives on the grammar, which remains unpredictable throughout the sentence. In the first clause, for example, as it is first read, 'Breaking earth upon a spring-haired elbow' may be taken, grammatically, in two ways: as a bound (dependent) clause, equivalent to 'while it was breaking earth...', or as a nominal group in which 'breaking' modifies 'earth', equivalent to 'earth which was breaking...' More formally:[17]

(a) **Bound clause**

Predicator	Complement	Adjunct
Breaking	earth	upon a spring-haired elbow

(b) **Nominal group**

Modifier	Head	Qualifier
Breaking	earth	upon a spring-haired elbow

The fact that (a) is the appropriate interpretation only emerges as the sentence unfolds, much as the resolution of a narrative mystery does, at the level of discourse, in a mystery novel.

Clauses	Interpretation
(a) Breaking earth upon a spring-haired elbow	The intruder, a god is breaking earth upon a spring-haired elbow.
(b) lone	he is alone
(c) a palm beyond head-grains	and there is a palm beyond head-grains
(d) a guard of prim fronds	which is like a guard of prim fronds
(e) piercing high hairs of the wind	and the high hairs pierce the wind
(f) as one who bore the pollen highest	like someone who bore the pollen highest
(g) Blood-drops in the air above the even belt of tassels, above the coarse leaf teasing on the waist	and there are blood-drops in the air...
(h) steals the lone intruder	the lone intruder steals in
(i) tearing wide the chaste hide of the sky	and he tears wide...

The grammar is also often elliptical, and not always clarified by the distribution of commas. The following table indicates the grammatical 'narrative' of the poem, also the narrative of the sun rising. This leaves the problem of thesis untouched; that is, what it is that is being pointed to when the poet says 'spring-haired elbow' and so on. But if the 'lone intruder' is taken to be 'a god', mentioned in line 13, the arrest does have the artistic point of miming the slow establishment of sunrise. First the sun itself is not immediately present. It shows its effects before it assumes ascendancy. The progression of the sentence is masked a number of times by the lack of finite verbs. Nominal structures such as (b), (c), (d), (g) and (a) on one interpretation, suspend the units in the sentence, without clear grammatical connections, hence direction. This is particularly clear with the *suspended* 'blood-drops in the air' which is emphasised by the parallelism of 'above' at the ends of lines 7 and 8, but each of these structures can be seen as a dramatisation of the idea of suspense. The relations which the reader surmises among these structures can be shown in performance, which can give a temporal direction to them while leaving the grammatical ties still tacit. The grammatical idea of 'suspense', 'waiting', with its sexual overtones, can be preserved, while the voice mimes the actual temporal onset of dawn, or consummation, which is articulated in the second sentence, from lines 12 to 14, in a non-finite clause, which refers but cannot comment.

These brief comments on 'Dawn', inadequate as they are, especially on the puzzle of the lexis in the poem, may illustrate the general point about poetic discourse as conventionally requiring a reader to look into the language. The reader of 'Post Mortem' may make some kind of sense of the text without grasping it as a poem, but if he is to read it as a poem he needs to focus on the text as such at the level of discourse. The reader of 'Dawn', however, will not be able to make even elementary sense of the text without looking into the language, that is by taking it as a poem. *Both of these texts, if they are to be read as poems* require imaginative participation by the reader. 'Dawn' wears its poeticality on its sleeve because form (grammar and vocabulary) are highlighted, while to some extent that of 'Post Mortem' is concealed.

These comments on 'Post Mortem' and 'Dawn' are not by any means exhaustive, and are not intended as defences of 'obscurity', nor are they based on a whole-hearted admiration of all aspects of the poems. At present, African poetry in English stands at a crossroads: we need to draw on the discoveries and ideas produced by poets like Soyinka, who does pose very fundamental questions about poetry as a verbal art, and cannot be dismissed on the grounds that his poems are difficult to understand at a first reading, or eurocentric.[18] Although contemporary younger

African poets will not want to copy all Soyinka's methods, they will be unwise simply to dismiss them with catchphrases and avoidances. An interest in poetry begins with an interest in the workings of language, a fascination with, and an endless patience with the ramifications of words and the process of thought. It may be that of all types of text, poetry comes closest to revealing this.[19] This fascination with the revelation and endless ramifications of words is not alien to political understanding. On the contrary it is fundamental to it.[20] Nor is it true that all traditional oral poetry is simple, direct and easy to understand. The way Soyinka manipulates conventional English grammar in 'Dawn' is akin to the methods Babalola ascribes to the ijala poet.

the construction of each ijala sentence should be different, at least slightly different, from that of its ordinary-speech counterpart.[21]

A poet working towards a kind of poetry which is simple in its grammar, and accessible in its vocabulary, and which has a different ideological outlook from Soyinka's, needs to bear in mind the insights of his work, and that of other African modernist poets. This essay has been directed towards trying to see what may be useful from this point of view in Soyinka's technique.

NOTES

1   Idanre (New York: Hill and Wang, 1967), p. 31.

2   *Ibid.* p. 9.

3   Chinweizu, Onwuchekwa Jemie and Ihechukwu Madubuike, *Towards the Decolonization of African Literature*, Volume 1 (Enugu: Fourth Dimension Press, 1980), pp. 167–72.

4   Georg M. Gugelberger, 'Marxist Literary Debates and their Continuity in African Literary Criticism' in Georg Gugelberger (ed.), *Marxism and African Literature* (London: James Currey, 1985), pp. 1–20.

5   See Glossary.

6   Halliday explains the three macrofunctions and their typical realisations in 'Modes of Meaning and Modes of Expression' in D.J. Allerton, Edward Carney, and David Holdcroft (eds), *Function and Context in Linguistic Analysis: Essays Offered to William Haas* (Cambridge: Cambridge University Press, 1979), pp. 57–79. See also the Glossary.

7   See Chapter 1 for further comments on poetic conventions.

8   Wole Soyinka, *Myth, Literature and the African World* (Cambridge: Cambridge University Press, 1976), p. 6.

9   See, for example N.J. Udeoyop, *Three Nigerian Poets* (Ibadan: Ibadan University Press, 1973), pp. 42–3; and *Myth, Literature and the African World*, p. 10.

10   English explanations of deconstructionism can be found in Jonathan

Culler, *On Deconstruction: Theory and Criticism after Structuralism* (London: Routledge and Kegan Paul, 1983), and *The Deconstructive Turn* by Christopher Norris (London: Methuen, 1983).

11 *Myth, Literature and the African World*, p. 6.

12 *Ibid.* pp. 53–4.

13 The issue is incisively discussed in J.Z. Kronenfeld, 'The "Communistic" African and the "Individualistic Westerner"' in Bernth Lindfors (ed.), *Critical Perspectives on Nigerian Literature* (Washington DC: Three Continents, 1979), pp. 237–64)

14 Per Wästberg (ed.), *The Writer in Modern Africa* (The Scandinavian Institute of African Studies, 1968), pp. 20–21

15 *Ibid.* p. 21

16 This concept is taken from John McH. Sinclair's paper 'Lines about "Lines"' in Ronald Carter (ed.), *Language and Literature* (London: Allen and Unwin, 1982), pp. 163–73.

17 The terminology is taken from Halliday's systemic functional grammar. The bound clause functions as a part of a sentence or 'clause complex'; while the nominal group, or word-group clustered about a noun, functions as part of a clause, usually as its subject or complement/object. See Glossary, under 'Group'.

18 *The Decolonization of African Literature*, pp. 163–238.

19 See Chapter 1.

20 See Chapter 1.

21 Adeboye Babalola, 'Ijala Poetry among the Oyo-Yoruba' in Uchegbulam K. Abalogu, Garba Ashiwaju, Regina Amadi-Tshiwala (eds), *Oral Poetry in Nigeria* (Lagos: Nigeria Magazine, 1981), p. 11.

CHAPTER 3

Okigbo's Technique in 'Distances I'

The following commentary deals with 'Distances I' from the point of view of Christopher Okigbo's handling of reference, allusion, textual unity, and speech acts. But it begins with some preliminary remarks by way of justification, since Okigbo's work has been the subject of much polemic. He is said to be obscure, unAfrican, elitist, and to rely too heavily on an unassimilated modernism derived from the American poets, Ezra Pound and T.S. Eliot.[2] The last charge, when directed at the earlier books of *Labyrinths*, is well founded, but in the 'middle' work, which includes 'Distances', Okigbo transcends his earlier imitativeness and writes some of his best pieces.[3] 'Distances' is a significant sequence in that it provides the philosophical centre to Okigbo's quest. The other charges – of obscurity, unAfricanness, and elitism – are in some ways understandable but fundamentally confused in conception.

Okigbo's central philosophical idea deeply involves modernity and its mixture of clash and mesh with his traditions. Okigbo adopts a modernist technique as his way of articulating that radical undercutting of older foundations and certainties that even the fullest independence cannot reinstate. True, Okigbo derives his style from the West, but two points must be remembered about this: first, that the imagist method he uses came to the West itself largely from China and Japan, or rather, as Chinese and Japanese poetry were understood by western poets; second, that modernist verse is not the monopoly of elitist and/or capitalist-orientated poets. The communists Mayakovski, Macdiarmid and Neruda all employ modernist styles; and in the first phase of Bolshevik rule, modernist art and literature were equated in their radical disruptiveness and their subversion of received (bourgeois) canons as a further expression of the political revolution. It is with the rise of Joseph Stalin and the demise of the original conception of the 'soviet' that doctrines of writing which in effect went back to nineteenth-century (bourgeois) realism became 'official', and modernism was seen by Lukàcs as a symptom, not now of radical departure, but of bourgeois decadence. Nor should it be forgotten that Brecht's style was affected by his study of Chinese and Japanese poetry and drama.

Okigbo's obscurity is attacked now by African critics who count themselves of the left as well as those who take up a culturalist position. From the left he is criticised for the same reasons that Lukàcs attacked Joyce and Kafka or the surrealist poets of the 1920s. While this criticism has stimulated an interest in forging a radical popular poetry – with all the technical problems that brings – it would be a mistake to take such poetry as the only kind worth reading, especially for the radical of the left. It may be argued that the 'simple' neo-Soviet kind of poetry is, in fact, more conservative, ultimately, than modernism. The latter is subversive of received commonsense[4] categories as encoded in habitual language usage, that is, of a dominant ideology. This common sense is, after all, what our rulers have taught us is normal and proper; but a seriously revolutionary poetry must help its audience to think and to perceive in new ways, not merely to invert or reshuffle the old 'certainties'. A poetry which questions norms is, almost by definition, philosophical and demands thought, but that does not necessarily make it 'elitist'.

The charge that Okigbo is obscure is often made, but what this obscurity might consist in is seldom examined. In fact, as will be shown, obscurity cannot be taken in an absolute way, as 'in' a poem, and as all of the same kind. Some of the sources of this obscurity can be seen from a close analysis of the poet's techniques. To this I now turn. Here is the poem itself.

DISTANCES I

FROM FLESH into phantom on the horizontal stone	1
I was the sole witness of my homecoming...	2
Serene lights on the other balcony:	3
redolent fountains bristling with signs –	4
But what does my divine rejoicing hold?	5
A bowl of incense, a nest of fireflies?	6
I was the sole witness to my homecoming...	7
For in the inflorescence of the white	8

chamber, a voice, from very far away,	9
chanted, and the chamber descanted, the birthday of earth,	10
paddled me home through some dark	11
labyrinth, from laughter to the dream.	12
Miner into my solitude,	13
incarnate voice of the dream,	14
you will go,	15
with me as your chief acolyte,	16
again into the anti-hill...	17
I was the sole witness to my homecoming...⁵	18

Representation⁶

Although Okigbo frequently does not refer to an immediate physical situation, we know from his introduction to *Labyrinths*⁷ that the scene in 'Distances' is an operating theatre. The scene is represented by the poet from the viewpoint of himself as a patient on the 'horizontal stone' or operating table, under anaesthetic; but also from time to time he observes himself from a position outside this particular experience, when in a chorus-like reiteration he says, 'I was the sole witness of my homecoming...' in lines 2, 7, and 18. At the same time, and in the same words used to refer to the operating table, Okigbo also refers to an inner dreamscape experienced by himself as a patient moving into unconsciousness. There is thus a double reference to an outer physical world and an inner psychic one. This is particularly clear at the beginning of the poem when the outer world is still near to consciousness. As the poet sinks from consciousness, the inner world, too, sinks deeper, becoming a traditional shrine and then, further into the psyche, a mythical landscape.

This double reference is realistically motivated, since it follows the course of an actual anaesthesia (a variation on the idea of the poet's vision being a dream). The first two lines set the double scene clearly enough: 'From flesh into phantom', from the bodily to the intangible and imagined, as if the body is dissolved and the utterer becomes a ghost. 'Phantom' has connotations of surgery too, as the term 'phantom limb' shows. In addition the word suggests the world of spirits and death, which anyone undergoing surgery feels much closer to than in his or her normal routines. In the same line Okigbo's metaphor of the 'horizontal stone' represents both the actual operating table and an altar, perhaps a pyre. That it is an altar is encouraged by the similar depictions in other parts of *Labyrinths*. For example, in 'Siren Limits IV' which, in some ways, preludes 'Distances', Okigbo writes,

> When you have finished
> & done up my stitches
> Wake me near the altar,
> & this poem will be finished[8]

And in the poem immediately following 'Distances I' he says,

> And in the freezing tuberoses of the white
> chamber, eyes that had lost their animal
> colour, havoc of eyes of incandescent rays,
> pinned me, cold, to the marble stretcher[9]

where the 'white chamber' is the scene of the 'marble' or stone 'stretcher'.

This first line, then, makes simultaneous reference to a modern operation and to an 'altar' in a traditional religious ceremony. In each situation, the poet lies passively under the ritual attendance of figures in special clothing, with specialised skills. The 'white chamber' is equally interpretable as a shrine or an operating theatre.

These very similarities, however, also highlight the contrast between modern scientific medicine and traditional worship. In his anesthetised fantasy, the speaker moves back, or 'down', to an earlier stage in his biography, to a pre-scientific and unwestern 'homecoming', an inner journey back in cultural time and individual experience. It is solitary because the experience, encompassed in the dream, is inaccessible to anyone else. The wanness of Okigbo's refrain, 'I am the sole witness to my homecoming', testifies to the fact that this homecoming in fantasy is by no means the same thing as an actual resumption of earlier norms or an earlier sense of cultural certainties. The refrain, too, comes from a voice which is not in the scenes 'within' the poem. It is an artistically self-conscious comment on the experiences of the poem as a whole, totalising, and addressed to a reader. It is, indeed, like a chorus.

The poem moves on to mention 'serene lights on the other balcony.' This also may have double reference, as the lights of the operating table, 'serene' because experienced with anesthetised vision, and also as the illuminations in the religious setting, in the 'white chamber' thought of as a shrine. 'Signs' may also be religious or scientific, either features of a religious ritual or evidence of the spiritual world, or in the scientific sense, screens, dials, charts, and so on. The 'divine rejoicing' represents, together with the 'laughter' of line 12, the effects of the gas and also a religious experience. 'Incense' also suggests religious ritual, but may also stand metaphorically for the scent of the gas; the speaker inhales both. The 'voice from very far away' is both priestly 'chant' and 'descant' and also the request and reply as the surgeon calls for this or that instrument whose name is repeated by the assistant who hands it to him, another ritual.

The operating theatre and the shrine, in modern terms, contrast with each other, but not in a traditional context, where they are not distinguished. Both spiritual and physical, science and spell, the older ritual aims at a more comprehensive kind of healing than does surgery. Okigbo's inner journey begins, naturalistically, in the modern medical world and moves toward what is both deeper and nearer to his youth. The return to the traditional shrine might seem to comprise the 'homecoming'; but such an interpretation is premature, because the journey continues, deeper than the individual biography or the particular culture, till it comes to a fundamental, mythical ambience, which may be related to Jung's 'collective unconscious' in which certain mythical stereotypes, the 'archetypes', are said by Jung to express the deepest levels of the human mind, beyond any particular culture. For Jung, civilisation depends on the individual's gaining this contact with archetypal images. In presenting this idea Okigbo is not, of course, necessarily committed either to an adherence to Jung's notions or to the idea that any actual man can really live outside, or beyond, a specific society. The poetic image represents an impossible archimedean point which may be imagined in order to throw actual lives and cultures into sharper perspective, and thus to bring out their contingence. One of the unsettling and radical insights Okigbo brings his reader to, is that the norms, values, the 'natural' and the 'commonsense' with which we were brought up, and as children took to be absolute, are not so. This insight cannot be disassociated from 'modernity', and it is fundamental to modernism and postmodernism in the arts.

This double reference is primarily a matter of individual words, of lexis, and of Okigbo's relative lack of naturalistic description, as can be seen from the fact that a reader who had not read the introduction to *Labyrinths* could be forgiven for not guessing that the poem refers to an operation. In this sense the text is obscure, and the obscurity is the price paid for the insights revealed by the double reference in this text. Double reference is not intrinsically obscure, however, since it is basically merely a development of the ordinary conversational pun.

Allusion[10]

After line 4 the double reference becomes more sporadic, and Okigbo relies more on allusion to mark out his mythical journey. The double reference can still be felt in the 'voice, from very far away', but this voice now begins to carry the reader forward, allusively, into the mythical landscape – 'paddled me home through some dark/labyrinth' – on a journey by water. The allusion appears to be to *The Epic of Gilgamesh*,[11] which Okigbo suggests elsewhere by mention of the names of various gods and men in that myth. Here the connection is more tenuous, but a number of factors suggest it.

Gilgamesh himself makes a journey to the land of death, and it ends in failure, like Okigbo's 'journey of several centuries from Nsukka to Yola in pursuit of what turned out to be an illusion'.[12] The illusion in Gilgamesh's case is the belief that a man may achieve immortality by dint of effort and determination. He too makes a journey over water in this quest and meets the figure of Utnapishtim, who is known as 'The Faraway' a name echoed in the 'voice from very far away' which guides Okigbo here, as Utnapishtim acts as the guide of Gilgamesh. Furthermore, Utnapishtim tells Gilgamesh that the gods had decreed that he, Utnapishtim, should 'live in the distance',[13] again echoing Okigbo's poem, this time its title. Perhaps too, in the earlier part of the poem, the Gilgamesh motif is foreshadowed in the 'horizontal stone', which has been interpreted as an operating table and an altar, but it is also similar to a sarcophagus, which is associated with the journey into death in the ancient Egyptian cosmology. This sarcophagus is mentioned in 'Fragments out of the Deluge', and the title suggests the Middle Eastern myth of the flood which occurs in *The Epic of Gilgamesh* in a version which predates that of Genesis, Utnapishtim being the equivalent of Noah. Almost in the same breath, in 'Fragments out of the Deluge', Okigbo mentions Enkidu, the 'wild man' who, he says, is the 'companion and second self of Gilgamesh'.[14] This interpretation of Enkidu as Gilgamesh's alter ego is not to be found in the myth itself. It represents a modern psychoanalytical approach put forward by Jung in *Symbols of Transformation*, where he refers to 'the higher and lower man, egoconsciousness and shadow, Gilgamesh and Enkidu',[15] and says of this myth, that it 'could probably be paraphrased thus: just as man consists of a mortal and an immortal part, so the sun is a pair of brothers, one of whom is mortal, the other immortal'.[16] Gilgamesh, of course is identified by Jung as a 'sun hero'.

Just as Okigbo as the poet-hero ('sunbird') enters the underground realm of the labyrinth after a sea journey and comes to the 'anti-hill', so Gilgamesh makes a similar sea journey and comes to the mountain that leads to the underworld, symbolising, for Jung, the unconscious. This mountain is called 'Mashu', and Sandars notes, in his glossary, that it has twin peaks and is regarded as the place of the sun's return to the world in the dawn, and it was identified with the 'Anti-Lebanon Mountains'.[17] 'Anti-Lebanon' seems to be echoed in the otherwise very puzzling 'anti-hill'.

Perhaps enough has been said to establish prima facie a case for taking Okigbo's 'Distances I', whatever else it may suggest, to be intertextually connected to the Gilgamesh epic. This widens the significance of the poet's individual journey and suggests an intercultural dimension to what began as a personal confrontation with the unconscious and a visit to the kingdom of death. Okigbo refers on page 33 of *Labyrinths* to the Sumerian goddess of the underworld, Irkalla (or Ereshkigal). He presents an image of a universal psychic depth and, in this sense, a kind of 'home'. It suggests what Okigbo calls 'a nameless religion'.[18] There is, of course, every danger that what seems to be universal may turn out to be a western imposition or at least borrowing. But the process of the poem shows a progression from the concrete individual in the operating theatre to the first culture, and beyond; so that the archetypal in the end is presented in terms of, and reached through, the particular *contingent* culture. And the whole mission is placed in the mind of a specific African.

Textual Cohesion[19]

Characteristic of Okigbo's technique is the use of grammatically disjointed sentences, a technique particularly associated with modernism, especially imagism.

Sentence 1, for example, trails away into dots and is not overtly connected to sentence 2, which is moodless (without subject or finite verb) and also breaks off, this time in a dash. Two questions follow, which are related by their parallelism, sentences 3 and 4. Sentence 3 seems to be connected to sentence 2 by the conjunction 'But'. However, this is a slightly unusual type of 'but', since it is brought to bear by the fiat of the poet, rather than by the internal logic of the connection. The difference may be illustrated thus:

(1) He put on his hat. But it didn't fit.
(2) He put on his hat. But that was foolish.

In (2) 'But' is used to represent the speaker's judgement, while in (1) it marks the internal logic of the two sentences.

Sentence 5 breaks in on the second of these questions, sentence 4, and also ends in dots. Sentence 6 begins with a conjunctive 'For' similarly motivated to the 'But' in sentence 3 but more attenuated. A suggestion as to what 'For' ties with will be made in the next section.

The relation between sentences 7 and 6 is more straightforward than has been the case so far because they have the same topic, 'voice' for which 'miner' is an approximate synonym. But still there is no other connection besides this one through vocabulary. Then sentence 7 ends with more dots and is itself broken into by the refrain, sentence 6, closing the poem and ending in dots also.

The disjunction of sentence-connections has the effect of sending the reader the more intently back to the vocabulary, making him read it more imaginatively than he might otherwise, in order to find the dynamic 'thread' of meaning which makes the text a whole. The semantic relations among vocabulary items in any text has a cohesive function. The poem is not unusual in that. It is slightly unusual in its almost entire lack of other kinds of cohesion, and in that often the semantic connections between the cohesive items may not be immediately apparent; perceiving the 'lexical cohesion', as it is called, demands active imaginative participation by the reader.[20]

He begins to notice, for example, that 'miner' in sentence 7 is semantically related to 'labyrinths' in sentence 6, since both involve tunnelling and dark passageways. These are related to 'homecoming' in sentence 5, if the notion of home is taken in a psychological way as the 'hidden depths' of a person, and in a cultural sense that Okigbo will have in mind the actual labyrinth at Arochukwu. 'Homecoming' also occurs in sentences 1 and 8, and is itself connected to 'birthday' since usually the place of birth is taken as a person's home, and more obviously to 'home' in sentence 6. 'Voice' in sentence 7 harks back to sentence 6 which contains 'laughter', 'descanted' and 'chanted' which are all produced by the voice, the last two being associated with religion and so with 'acolyte' in sentence 6, and with 'incense' in sentence 4, and to 'voice' again in line 14. In sentence 7, also, 'dream' recalls 'dream' in sentence 6, 'serene' in sentence 2, and 'phantom' in sentence 1; and these are related contrastively to 'incarnate' in sentence 7, and 'flesh' in sentence 1, articulating the basic opposition in the text between the body in a particular time and place, inert, and the mind which moves a very long way out of it. The lexical cohesion is shown in Figure 1, in which one or two further items have been added. The reiteration of the refrain in lines 2, 7 and 18 is similar to lexical cohesion in being repetitive, but it is left out of account in Figure 1. It is dealt with in terms of speech acts, which take up the next section.

Speech Acts

The poem may also be looked at as a sequence of speech acts indicating the movement of the poet's interpersonal attitudes. Looking at the text this way merges its 'coherence' (a textual feature) and its 'interaction' (an interpersonal feature), though these are separable in theory. The intonations used by a performer would show the flow and wholeness of the poem in a 'musical' way, and would be based on the speech roles and the attitudes assumed by the 'I', which will be identified with Okigbo, for convenience.

Although the individual sentence is not necessarily the same as a unit of intonation, it does indicate fundamental aspects of speech role-playing;[21] and commentary at this degree of delicacy will serve to bring out the main lines of the interactional/textual flow of the poem as a succession of attitudes and roles with their own rhetorical 'logic'.

In the first sentence the poet (or performer representing 'I') speaks in the first-person role and adopts a totalising perspective about a past homecoming. The poet is, however, speaking in a performance-present and directly to his audience/reader. The overall experience is summed up in preparation for the more detailed exposition starting in the second sentence. The speech act performed in the first sentence may be labelled, annunciative revelation. In sentence 4 and then again in sentence 7, similar words are spoken, as a refrain. It is as if the poet alternates between the role of chorus, who always sees the quest as a whole, already complete, and the role of actor, whose knowledge is partial until the end when it may coincide with that of the chorus. The repetitions of the refrain change its significance as they accumulate. First, there is an annunciative force to it, then it becomes reassertive, and in the last line retrospective.

Sentence 2 is 'moodless' in that no person/subject is mentioned and it has no tense to indicate time in relation to the speaker and subject. Aspects of the scene are mentioned as visual impressions only, as it were. This serves to express lack of orientation in time and space, mirroring the floating experience of the patient sinking into his dream. In the third and fourth sentences the disorientation leads to self-questioning, a self-doubt which perhaps is also doubt about the status of the self. The speaker is

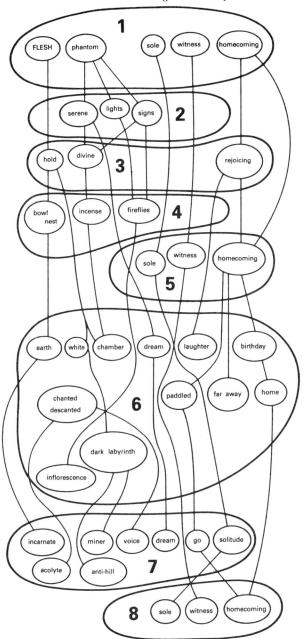

Figure 1: lexical cohesion in 'Distances I'

Numbers and heavy encircling lines indicate sentences. Finer lines indicate cohesive 'ties'.

orientated, in sentences 2 and 3/4 more directly to the narrative of his experience 'in' the poem, than to the reader, especially in sentences 3 and 4, where the questions obviously are not addressed to the reader, though he, of course, is a witness to the asking. The questioning self-doubt is set in the narrative past, but expressed in the present tense, like the articulating of the poet's thoughts at the time.

In sentence 5 the refrain returns, now reassertively. But having taken in the disorientation of the self in sentence 2, the reader will be more likely to 'underline' for himself the same theme as it is taken up in the refrain, since there too the notion of 'I' being a 'sole witness' to what 'I' is doing, puts in question the very status of the speaker's identity. How can someone witness himself, and furthermore be the *only* such witness? Sentence 6 follows on both from the refrain and from sentence 4, the self-doubt giving rise to a narrative explanation signalled by the inter-personally orientated cohesive item, 'For'. It switches to the third person, with the poet now in the role of observer in relation to the 'voice'. For the first time the 'I' of the poet (performer) takes a subsidiary position, recurring in line 11 as the predicated 'me', while 'voice' becomes the main topic and the subject. In sentence 6 the orientation is equally towards the reader and the self, since the poet is clarifying things to himself while telling the narrative to the reader, who has just been addressed directly in the refrain. In sentence 7 the speech role changes again, the poet now adopting a second-person position, and addressing the 'voice' in an assertion of commitment. This is a part of the narration, and so set in the past, but expressed in the future tense. This tone of commitment, contrasts with the earlier disorientations and self-questionings. It matches the (more detached) definiteness of the refrain, which comes back in sentence 8 to end the poem. It now flows out of the accumulated narrative of the poet's dream, and out of the previous refrains.

Once the poem has been understood at the level of discourse as interactive/textual coherence, a performance can be worked out which brings out these shifts in role and speech act, and makes the poem flow as a rhetorical rather than a logical whole, indeed as a miniature drama with its chorus and characters. The speech-act unity of poems as expressed in performance (especially in intonation) has been little studied as yet,[22] possibly because critics tend to think in terms of the written page, and possibly because those aspects of sound they do take into consideration, such as rhyme and stress, are to be found at definite points in the text, while intonation is not; it is cumulative and overarches other more atomistic units of language. In this overarching lies its unifying function, a kind of unifying which is more often associated with music. Discourse analysis along the lines developed by Burton, holds out some promise for a description of this flow in a poem, but as yet will not cover the kinds of distinctions assumed in Figure 2. In this the arrows represent a rhetorical connection which can be glossed as 'gives rise to'.

Conclusion

The techniques used by Okigbo – double reference, allusion, the development of an 'emotional unity' – do not of themselves produce obscurity. They are all used in everyday conversation. What makes Okigbo's text difficult to understand is the unfamiliarity, for a good many of his readers, of what he refers or alludes to. Obviously the poem would be plainer if Okigbo had made direct reference to an operating table, drawn an overt comparison between the ritual in the operating theatre, and the events in his 'dream', and if he had mentioned Gilgamesh and Anti-Lebanon, and so forth. But, for readers who do happen to be familiar with these cognate texts,[23] the indirections cause no obstacle to communication. And, as in conversation, there are rhetorical advantages to be had in the use of these indirections.

Take the following example from a poem by the Nigerian poet Idi Bukar, which alludes to the execution of 'coup plotters' in March 1986, and to the 1983 election-rigging by 'the Trickster'.

> He who'd managed his magic coup
> with pieces of printed paper
> and clever ways of counting
> now felt the Desert wind on his face happily
>
> They shot ten other people instead.[24]

Not everyone will understand the double reference, to 'the Desert' as a spiritual and social emptiness, or the allusion to the 'ten other people'. Those who will understand it are listeners to the radio, readers of the newspapers, in Nigeria, and those who can understand English and have a knowledge of poetic language.

To the foreigner the passage will be as obscure as is Okigbo's poem to the reader who has no experience of texts connected to operating theatres, Jung, or the *Epic of Gilgamesh*. Different cognate texts are connected to different ways of life and some are much more widely known, hence more public, than others which may indeed be accessible only to the leisured and expensively educated. To many African readers Okigbo's topic and the scatter of cognate texts in 'Distances I' will appear 'out of

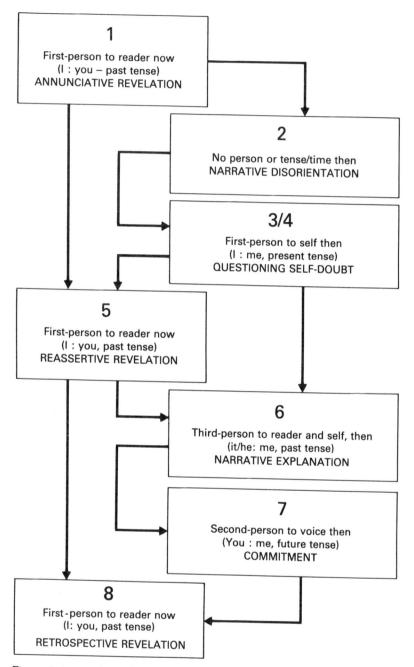

Figure 2: interactive coherence of 'Distances I'

the way'. Educated African Marxists such as Onoge[25] assume from some of Okigbo's comments about poetry that he is concerned only with 'art for art's sake' and so irrelevant to the African left. In addition, the psychoanalytical approach to Marxist socialism has not, as yet, gained much ground in Africa. Yet Okigbo's work lends itself to the post-Brechtian and postmodernist approaches to poetry which have grown up in the West, since Okigbo's death and which challenge the somewhat static theories of socialist realism. The leftist dismissal of Okigbo is unfortunate since surely his insight into modernity and the contingency of cultures and the individual subject does have a bearing on, and can make a contribution to, the understanding of neocolonial Africa, once this interpretation goes beyond a certain level. Okigbo's poetry is philosophical and intellectual, of course, but it is a sad and lame 'Marxism' that cannot accommodate that.

NOTES

1 Christopher Okigbo, *Labyrinths* (London: Heinemann, 1971), p. 53.

2 The attack from the culturalist viewpoint is perhaps the best known. See Chinweizu, Onwuchekwa Jemie, and Ihechukwu Madubuike, *Towards the Decolonization of African Literature, Volume I* (Enugu: Fourth Dimension, 1980), which concentrates on the poems written before *Path of Thunder*. For Marxist criticism, see Omafume F. Onoge, 'The Crisis of Consciousness in Modern African Literature: A Survey (1974)' in Georg M. Gugelberger (ed.), *Marxism and African Literature* (London: James Currey, 1985) pp. 21–45. Okigbo is mentioned on p. 34 in relation to 'art for art's sake' and 'poesie pure'. For different approaches to Okigbo's technique from the one taken in this essay, see Donatus Nwoga, 'Obscurity and Commitment in Modern African Poetry' in *African Literature Today* 9 (1974) pp. 26–45, and Romanus Egudu, 'Anglophone African Poetry and Vernacular Rhetoric: The Example of Okigbo', in *Lagos Review of English Studies*, Volume 1, No. 1 (1979), pp. 104–13.

3 A view from which Goodwin dissents. See Ken Goodwin, *Understanding African Poetry* (London: Heinemann, 1982), pp. 42–3.

4 Gramsci counterposes static 'common sense' with philosophical thinking that questions its categories, and which working people need to develop if social change is to come about at a radical level, and hence be lasting. Thus philosophy is not taken to be intrinsically elitist. See Antonio Gramsci, *The Modern Prince and Other Writings* (New York: International Publishers, 1957), pp. 56–7.

5 See note 1.

6 From the linguistic point of view the representational or 'ideational' function of language contrasts with the 'interpersonal' and the 'textual' functions. See Glossary.

7 *Labyrinths*, p. xii.

8 *Ibid.*, p. 17.

9 *Ibid.*, p. 54.

10 Allusion is a non-referential way of relating a text to others, the phenomenon of 'intertextuality'. See Glossary. The term 'allusion' is used where the intertextual connection is to be specially drawn attention to in some way; any lexical item has a potential for occurring in other texts, and in that sense is allusive. Allusion resembles lexical cohesion, except that it is orientated away from the particular text (exophoric), while lexical cohesion is internally orientated (endophoric).

11 N.K. Sandars (ed./tr.) *The Epic of Gilgamesh* (Harmondsworth: Penguin, 1972). This translation was first published in 1960 and may thus have been known to Okigbo. The Gilgamesh theme emerges overtly in 'Fragments from the Deluge' (1961–2) but in a footnote Okigbo connects the death of Enkidu to the lioness who is mentioned in 'Siren Limits' (1961). In the Epic itself, according to Sandars, Enkidu is killed by an undescribed monster, Humbaba; though Gilgamesh himself is associated with the lion, as a killer of lions, as he kills Humbaba.

12 *Labyrinths*, p. xi.

13 *The Epic of Gilgamesh*, p. 113.

14 *Labyrinths*, p. 28.

15 C.J. Jung, *Symbols of Transformation* (Routledge and Kegan Paul, 1965), p. 437.

16 *Ibid.*, p. 202.

17 *The Epic of Gilgamesh*, p. 123.

18 *Labyrinths*, p. 58.

19 Cohesion is the way in which individual words 'tie' with each other semantically to provide the 'thread' of meaning in a text. The treatment here follows M.A.K. Hallliday and Ruqaiya Hasan, *Cohesion in English* (London: Longman, 1976) and confines analysis to cohesive ties between sentences. This is but a convenience since cohesion is semantic, not grammatical – that is, not a kind of grammar above the rank of sentence.

20 See the comparison of a poem to a conversational turn, in Chapter 1, pp. 1–3. 'Coherence' may be distinguished from 'cohesion' by the lack of manifest lexical markers of textual continuity.

21 The 'mood' of a free clause indicates whether the speaker is asking a question, making a comment, or issuing an order or request. The mood of the free clause in a sentence with a number of other, dependent, clauses, is the one that decides the mood of the sentence, or clause-cluster, as a whole. This fairly crude analysis of mood, or speech-act, can be made more subtle, as can be seen from the capacity of an imperative clause to express commands, requests, pleas, and variations of each; but to do this the analysis has to take into account the level of discourse, and the expressive force of intonation. The 'interpersonal' layer of discourse is to be contrasted with the 'ideational' and the 'textual', already looked at as representation and cohesion/allusion.

22 See Chapter 6.

23 See Glossary, and also a treatment of intertextuality in Chapter 9.

24 Idi Bukar, *First the Desert Came and Then the Torturer* (Zaria: Rag Press, 1986), p. 36. Shehu Shagari, the 'Trickster' politician, was widely believed to have rigged the 1983 election, and was overthrown in January 1984 by General Buhari, himself removed by General Babangida in 1985. The latter eventually freed Shagari, and claimed to have forestalled a coup-plot, led by General Mamman Vatsa, who with nine others, was executed by firing squad.

25 *Op.cit.* in note 1.

CHAPTER 4

Song and Copy: the Relation between Oral and Printed in Kofi Awoonor's 'Dirge'

'Dirge' is a poem written within the school which sees the African oral poem – or 'song' as it will be called here for convenience[1] – as the best basis of modern printed African poetry in English or English translation. The printed poem will be called the 'copy'. This school is represented by such poets as Okot p'Bitek, Mazisi Kunene, Gabriel Okara, and Kofi Awoonor himself; and it is usually contraposed to the more print-based poetry of such composers as Soyinka and Okigbo. The poets of this school do not hold identical views about the relation between copy and song, nor about the position of English; but all emphasise the importance to them of some use of song techniques in their poetry, and all deal in one way or another with English as a translation language, and with the question of 'Africanness' in relation to it.

The difference between a song and a copy have been well stressed in such well-known works as Ruth Finnegan's *Oral Poetry*[2], and in association with the poets of this school, by such writers as Heron[3], Chinweizu et al.[4], Awoonor[5], and Okot p'Bitek[6]. What has not so far been examined is the nature of the relationship between a copy and a song when the copy alludes through its style to song as a genre. We then get a transposition from oral to printed modes and the different styles typical of the two genres are brought into interaction; we *read* what has many characteristics of something composed to be *heard*. We see the song through the copy. Any copy poem which alludes to song will carry this relation, but 'Dirge' is a particularly striking case because the copy is a very close mime of a song, and could pass as a printed translation into English from Ewe. This is the copy.

DIRGE[7]

(To be sung to slow drumbeats of ten-second intervals)

Tell them tell it to them	1
That we the children of Ashiagbor's house	2
Went to hunt: when we returned,	3
Our guns were pointing to the earth,	4
We cannot say it; someone say it for us.	5
Our tears cannot fall,	6
We have no mouths to say it with.	7
We took the canoe, the canoe with sandload	8
They say the hippo cannot overturn	9
Our fathers, the hippo has overturned our canoe	10
We come home	11
Our guns pointing to the earth	12
Our mother, our dear mother	13
Where are our tears, where are our tears	14
Give us mouth to say it, our mother	15
We are on our knees to you	16
We are still on our knees	17

Awoonor's translations of Ewe traditional poets show that he values the link that may be made between the modern copy poet and the singer. His earliest practice shows it. In 'Songs of Sorrow', he writes:

I am on the world's extreme corner,
I am not sitting in the row with the eminent
But those who are lucky
Sit in the middle and forget...
I can only go beyond and forget.[8]

His own version of Akpalu's song, 'Five' as he numbers it, runs

I am on the world's extreme corner
I am not sitting in the row with the eminent
Those who are lucky sit in the middle
sitting and leaning against a wall
They say I came to search.
I, Vinoko, can only go beyond and forget.[9]

'Dirge' is not assumed to be a translation, but what follows is not much affected by whether it is or not. The poem shows clear mimesis of the oral mode and of the dirge genre as shaped by Akpalu[10]. The most obvious indication is the stage direction that the copy should be sung to drumbeats. Most readers will probably not carry out the instruction, but perhaps rather imagine it. It could be followed and the copy used as the 'script' for a dramatic performance; but this would not make it a fully oral *composition*. It has to be remembered that the features of song style are as much a function of the singer's as the hearer's role. Awoonor's poem is not provided with music and the stage direction is of the vaguest. The instruction to beat the drum at ten-second intervals is not tied to the speed at which the script is to be sung. There is a line-rhythm,[10] but how this is to fit in with the drumbeats is not possible to infer. Some way of accommodating the instruction could be devised, no doubt, but both this vagueness and the presentation of the poem in a printed volume encourage the view that what we have is a copy *alluding* to the song genre. In one way the script resembles the written translation of an African traditional song which has been extracted from its context of performance, or a Scottish border ballad now commonly read as a copy. The transposition of early song to later script is a usual part of the evolution of literate poetry. The English sonnet form derives historically from song and its metre from the demands of music. But there is a difference between Awoonor's kind of allusion and the evolutionary relation of sonnet to song. For one thing the sonnet has evolved into something distinctly written and writing has opened up new technical possibilities. A parallel in English literature to Awoonor's more deliberate backward allusion may be found in the 'Lyrical Ballads'.[11]

'Dirge' has other features of the song style, such as the use of grammatical parallelism and the relative lack of conceptual innovation. But let us first consider the central problem the song/copy link poses, the double shift from oral to written (transposition) and from Ewe to English (translation).

Translation often occurs between oral traditions, the 'same' song being found in Hausa and Fulfulde, or in English and Danish. But the translation of 'Dirge' crosses cultures which are much more dissimilar than the pairs just mentioned. The translated and transposed Ewe song is now open to, and indeed has been produced for, an audience which is not intimate with Ewe social and aesthetic norms. The canoe, the hippo, Ashiagbor, all require conscious interpretation for the stranger; the kind of interpretation he can accept will be shaped by his own different assumptions as a literate reader of English. He will also be aware of this fact; he will be aware that the copy is a mimed song – a song within a copy. He will be familiar with a world which is wider than that of the original (imaginary) singer of the song, and he will ask himself such philosophical questions as, What is the cosmology this poem fits into? What are the tacit presuppositions of the audience? These are questions which are not open to the singer himself. We can sum up the difference by saying that the literate reader (or the performer) has a more 'global' view of the song than could occur in an Ewe village performance. This at least would be a strong tendency.

To focus the position just outlined, two features of the style will be examined, the use of parallelism and of pronouns. Parallelism is common in song and has been closely studied[12]. It is not peculiar to oral poetry; and all verse may be thought of as ultimately based on 'parallelism' of one sort or another.[13] But in much oral poetry parallelism is particularly prominent and often grammar-based. In lines 5, 7 and 15, of 'Dirge' we have adroitly varied repetitions of the idea of being unable to express emotion, and all containing 'say it'.

5a We				cannot	say it
5b	Someone				say it	for us
7 We		have no	mouths	to say it with
15		Give us mouth		to say it

For the singer/performer parallelism is functional: it helps him compose as he sings by providing a framework, time to think, and aids his memory when he repeats the performance. He cannot turn pages back or cross out, nor can his audience. But the reader with the printed copy before him will not need the repetition in the same way. He can turn or look back. He will be aware that the technique is *drawn from* song, and an allusion to it. It now forms part of the meaning of the poem and is no longer, either, shaped by the requirements of oral composition. The copy poet is asking the reader (or an audience in performance) to think himself back into older (deeper) ways of experiencing grief, and does so as part of a belief that modern African poetry should underline this relation. A contemporary reader will be all the more aware of this gesture if he knows something of the poetry which this poem and others like it implicitly turn against: the English literary tradition. And if he knows Awoonor's own position in modern African poetry the didactic force of this allusion will be all the stronger.

A second facet of the relation between copy and song can be seen if we look at the way Awoonor handles pronouns. The first-person plural ('we' and 'us') occurs ten times, referring to the singer and the audience collectively, and it expresses[14] the emotion of solidarity in grief. The reader of the copy does not, of course, feel himself as closely included as do the (imagined) participants in the performance. The reader sees the participants as fictive characters saying 'we'. He is an observer at one remove from the performance. This would be true if the copy were an actual translation of an actual song about an actual grief. Still the reader has access to the song only through the print. The situation depicted in an actual performance is known independently of that performance by the participants. For the reader, the imagined situation depends completely on those aspects of it picked out for verbal mention by the writer. He has no check. The oral text interprets a situation; the written one both interprets and creates one.

The copy lacks the immediacy of song, and the audience of a copy is more diffuse. It is drawn from those people scattered over the globe who buy books of written English poetry. The lack of emotional immediacy is obvious. The reader will not find himself in tears, or his voice cracking with emotion as he reads aloud. Secondary orality – perhaps a theatrical performance – may produce these symptoms but the situation is still fictive, the emotion still put on. There is no actual death. A recital can heighten the *expression* of emotion since this is typically related to (spoken or sung) tunes. The poem can be seen as a pattern of pleas and confessions, speech acts which have direct intonational implication for a spoken performance (as can be seen if we try to imagine the pleas delivered in the tone of commands, for example), as also for any melody[15].

But still in a performance the death being mentioned remains as remote as in a silent reading. This brings us to a second point about the pronouns, the fact that the death is not referred to directly. 'We' is the type of pronoun which always refers to a situation which is actually, or imagined to be, 'outside' the text, to the speaker him/herself and other relevant people. In the (fictive) performance there would be no need to specify who 'we' are, because it would be obvious. But 'it' differs from 'we' being typically used either to refer (back or forward) to something specified in the text, or to something already known to the participants. In the song 'it' in the first line refers forward to the fact

> That we the children of Ashiagbor's house
> Went to hunt: when we returned
> Our guns were pointing to the earth...

which refers obliquely to whatever the bereavement is, the hunting and returning metaphor itself having a pronoun-like reference to the actual situation never specified. Indirectly, then, all the instances of 'it' in the text refer to something, someone's death *as if it were* shared knowledge between the reader and the writer – a typical literary device used to 'draw a reader into' a text. But the type of reference which assumes shared common knowledge of a situation is, when not used in this 'dummy' literary way, typical of speech.[16]

For the reader 'it' and 'we' are used similarly in the sense that from neither can he identify what or who is being referred to except by a deduction from the title.

For the reader, or for the audience in a dramatised performance, 'it' remains remote because it remains a reference to an imaginary bereavement. The cause of grief is not specified. But the lack of specific reference has the opposite effect in a real oral performance. Here everyone knows who has died and how, and the very fact that they fail to mention it and do not wish to be more explicit, creates a strong bond of solidarity, and so enhances the immediacy of the emotional impact. The song (within the poem) is designed for this. The 'it' can refer to any death which requires a dirge, and will have different content each time the song is sung[17]. Furthermore, from the point of view of rhetoric, the idea of the singer's attempt to express the inexpressible is conveyed by the poet's refusal to be specific.

The reader and the singer see the situation, the death, at different removes. Not only does the reader have *more* interpreting to do, his interpretation is likely to be different. His perspectives are cosmopolitan; his experience as a reader of poetry will encourage him to see implicit generalisations. Awoonor himself suggests one in his narrative work, *This Earth, My Brother*. At the end of a passage describing the hypocritical followers of Nkrumah, the 'illiterate bank managers whose relatives are in the government' (note the sense given to 'illiterate'), we read:

> My death is remembered among these alien gravestones. For we, the children of Ashiagbor's house, went to hunt. When we returned our guns were pointing to the earth[18]

The idea of the metaphorical 'death' of a culture, of what is now modern Ghana, is suggested by the context, and indeed the tone of the book.

> Our sadness itself based upon that distant sadness which is the history of this land, defies all consolation[19]

just as does the grief of the mourners in 'Dirge'.

The reader, with a wider consciousness of modern Ghana and modern Africa sees the village dirge as an image of a much wider loss, as a speechlessness which may be interpreted as the loss of the ability to be sad, to realise that there is cause for sorrow. The very categories of meaning which might articulate the modern plight are no longer available because they are to be found in traditions that have been lost sight of. This, at least, seems to be Awoonor's point of view as the writer, seeing poetry of all kinds, as he does, as a necessary transformation and unification of the observable and unobservable world[20]

For him a poet enjoys

a closer link with the earth. As society progresses, this whole techno-logical society in which we are living today, we tend to forget about those other mysterious areas of human experience.[21]

For Awoonor, then, the relatively global perspectives of the modern reader and writer allow them to see the song (within the copy) as an image of the spiritual death of African traditions. The reader's role in relation to this poem is as far as possible to immerse himself in a mystical reunion with the Ancestors and the earth, participating imaginatively in the 'original' song rites and so, in some sense not entirely clear, to be revitalised. In the context the poem enacts a return to specific gods and psychic truths. But this view of art is by no means specifically African. It can be found in Carl Jung, for example, whose 'archetypes' correspond, as psychic-cum-primal beings, to Awoonor's Ancestors.

The creative process...consists in the unconscious activation of an archetypal image... By giving it shape, the artist translates it into the language of the present *and so makes it possible for us to find our way back to the deepest springs of life*... The artist seizes on this image, and in raising it from deepest unconsciousness he brings it into relation with conscious values, thereby transforming it until it can be accepted by the minds of his contemporaries according to their powers.[22]

The English reader may also think of D.H. Lawrence. The metapho-rical – the poetic – truth of Jung's and Awoonor's (and Lawrence's) statements, the need in some sense to get to the 'deep structures' of our experience, especially our emotional experience, which is indeed all too often subject to mental and physical repression, is not to be denied. But consider a different view of the poem, one which opens out to a reader, since a reader, because of his relative detachment, has far greater scope for imaginative interpretation than does the participant in the perfor-mance of the song.

Although it may be argued that the reader should respect the com-poser's interpretation, nothing forces him to, and nothing guarantees that the poet is necessarily conscious of the full meaning of his work.[23] Indeed Awoonor appears to forget that his own view of poetry is learned and sophisticated, even perhaps a kind of primitivism. It is the modern educated African who finds spiritual loss all around him, who goes with his tape-recorder to *preserve* the songs of old men and write books about them in English. Awoonor has learnt about poetry not only from Ewe singers but also from the printed word, the underlining of passages and the turning back of pages. This is 'technological' in that it is made possible by print[24].

Both Jung's and Awoonor's views are responses to the spiritual death which modern capitalism brings, to what Awoonor refers to as 'this whole technological society'. The effects are different, of course, as Ghana and Switzerland are different. Yet they nevertheless link the two cultures economically and historically in ways which inform the unequal daily lives of actual Swiss and Ghanaians. In their reactions to this force both Jung and Awoonor look inward and backward, but they do not, except dismissively, look immediately round them at the more concrete realisations of capitalism in the practical and mundane which makes the *spiritual* similarity between them seem all the more compelling. But just as the song always takes place in a specific village, is performed by particular people, who dance, drum, join in, so the copy too is situated in an actual place at an actual time.

The reader is sitting in a particular room with particular objects testifying to his income, class, social roles, family and biography. These things exemplify the relation the reader actually has to technology, which may be much more accommodating to it than views expressed just at a spiritual level suggest, and this relation will reveal sharp difference between the situation of an African and a Swiss intellectual. So to say that the reader of this poem is 'alone with the text' is misleading. The very capacity and opportunity to sit in private mark the reader socially, as does the ability to read English as a second language; as do the social purposes for which he reads – to pass tomorrow's examination, to write a paper, to commune with the Ancestors. Yet, in the context of African poetry in the English language the educational system is likely to loom large. While it may not account for all aspects of reading it is likely to shape responses in certain (perhaps examinable) ways, to encourage the printing and sale of the book in which the poem appears, to hold out promise of a comfortable life through literary critical proficiency. It is this dimension of reading (studying) that Awoonor's view of poetry turns away from. For him reading is a kind of concentration that blots out the surrounding actual world – something which the oral performer can hardly forget – and so underestimates the tacit force of the educational system in which most readers come across poetry[25].

Just as we are not bound to accept a person's own interpretation of his acts and utterances, so the reader need not accept Awoonor's own account of his poem. Although the text is constructed in such a way that we are encouraged to sympathise with and identify with the (imaginary) mourners, and to accept that they are on their knees to their ancestors, helpless and nonplussed with grief, the way in which we see this whole situation may well not be empathetic. We may see the characters, 'we', as indeed lost, and indeed distraught. Indeed 'it' has happened; modern Ghana (modern Nigeria) is 'dead'. But we may now see the participants' crisis as the more deepened, the solution the more hidden than ever from them, by their very turning back to the past, as a desperate and irrational response to bewilderment. And on this interpretation we see 'we' as victims whose plight we can feel for, but whose viewpoint we do not share, which we might hope to change.

Awoonor's view of the poem implies a criticism of modern education in the English manner since it is part of 'this whole technological society', a fundamental part. Paradoxically the backward- and inward-looking view of art fits more peaceably into such an 'ideological state apparatus'[26] than a view which takes account of the actual situation of reading. While the backward and inward view may be traditionally African in the sense that in Awoonor's hands it has African dramatis personae – ancestors rather than archetypes – it finally provides an ironic commentary on many an actual ritualising student. The prostration before the dispensers of wisdom, the verbal formulas and rites of passage into the motor car and fridge life – all these show an *acceptance of* (scramble for) modern technological and dependent capitalist ways of life. How many students seem to be crying:

Give us mouth to say it . . .
We are on our knees to you

not to their ancestors, but to the certificate-issuing gurus of 'this whole technological society'? And this way of looking at Awoonor's poem is itself only available to the literate student of the copy.

What has been said so far is perhaps no more than an elaboration of the truism that oral poetry does not have a 'literary criticism', and that printed poetry allocates great imaginative contribution to the communication to a reader[27]. Although this interpretation differs from Awoonor's, it does not constitute any adverse criticism of the technique; rather it aims to reveal the implications of using song as a model. Print adds density of meaning and width of implication without 'altering' the actual words used. The rules of discourse have been changed.[28]

The allusion to the oral tradition conveys an 'Africanness' in the sense that the particular model happens to be African and a reader can infer as much. There would, of course, be no need for an Ewe singer to suggest Africanness in his techniques. But the techniques used in English are not strikingly African. Translations from other oral traditions might well sound quite similar. Nor is Awoonor's aesthetic peculiarly African. Perhaps the vital Africanness of the poem consists in the fact that here is an African poet innovating, turning English in a way that has not been done before, making a verse which is technically distinct from typical English verse. The technique of this poem, and of others in the same school, represents a gain in that it provides a framework for verse composition which is neither an imitation of English metres (based on British pronunciation) nor 'free verse', which in the hands of many African poets constitutes a shelving of the problems of *verse* altogether. The grammatical parallelism of 'Dirge' is independent of pronunciation, and in the hands of a skilled craftsman such as Awoonor allows access to kinds of meaning, typical of poetry, which come from linguistic constraint.

The song model also makes comprehension easier, especially for a hearer; but there are other ways of achieving that. More important is the way the song model reasserts the role of emotional meaning in poetry. African modernists such as Soyinka and Okigbo appear 'dry' to many readers mainly because of their preoccupation with philosophical meaning which is seldom, as it were, dissolved in feeling. In song the expression of immediate emotion is both prominent and disciplined; and taking song as a model constitutes a reminder that poetry needs to fuse deep thought with deep feeling in the act of speech. The danger with the model may be that the balance may shift too far in the direction of expression of emotion, so that we get passionate presentation of the philosophically naive. The danger is inherent in the model since traditional oral poetry tends to reinforce communally-accepted norms uncritically. To do this in a copy poem is surely to throw away the gains to be had from literacy, which is more orientated towards the future and to change than is orality[29]. Awoonor's poem, like many others in this school, is both printed and (by allusion) oral; the fullest development of this style of poetry requires the composer to draw as richly as he can from *both* resources.

NOTES

1 I ask the reader to bear with this shorthand. While it is accurate as a description of Akpalu's Ewe poems, it is not safe, of course, to generalise that oral poetry is always sung, nor that what is sung is necessarily oral poetry. Isidore Okpewho, *The Epic in Africa: Towards a Poetics of Oral Performance* (Columbia University, 1979), pp. 154–5.

2 Ruth Finnegan, *Oral Poetry* (Cambridge: Cambridge University Press, 1977).

3 George Heron, *The Poetry of Okot p'Bitek* (London: Heinemann, 1976).

4 Chinweizu, Onwuchekwa Jemie, Ihechukwu Madubuike, *Towards the*

Decolonization of African Literature, Volume 1 (Enugu: Fourth Dimension Press, 1980).

5   Kofi Awoonor, *Guardians of the Sacred Word* (New York: Nok Publishers, 1974).

6   Okot p'Bitek, *Africa's Cultural Revolution* (London: Macmillan, 1973).

7   Kofi Awoonor and G. Adali-Morty (eds), *Messages from Ghana* (London: Heinemann, 1971).

8   Gerald Moore and Ulli Beier (eds), *Modern Poetry from Africa* (Harmondsworth: Penguin, 1968), p. 98.

9   Awoonor, *op. cit.* pp. 19–20.

10 Each line ends with a coincidence of grammatical and phonological boundaries, usually of clause and tone group, at least in my spoken recital. The line boundaries also tend to be reinforced by lexical and grammatical parallelism.

11 Like Awoonor, Wordsworth and Coleridge were trying to get away from an urbane kind of poetry which looked to a different culture, and to find models in the English and Scottish oral traditions.

12 See, for example Roman Jakobson, 'Grammatical Parallelism and its Russian Facet' in *Language*, volume 42, number 2 (1966); pp. 399–429 and 'Poetry of Grammar and Grammar of Poetry' in *Lingua*, Number 21 (1968), pp. 597–609.

13 The term 'parallelism' is restricted to prominent repetition of lexico-grammatical units. 'Poetry' is a qualitative term indicating intensity of meaning, while 'verse' refers to composition in 'lines', the lines being marked either by a pause (oral), or a margin-space (print), or both (script) when recited. 'Metre' refers to comparability of such lines from the point of view of their internal syllabic or stress structure. All poetry constrains the poet in some way and thus forces him into linguistic invention; this constraint can be defined with some confidence when it is a matter of metre or rhyme, less easily when it is matter of verse, and not at all easily when it is a matter of semantic depth. Okpewho illustrates nicely the way in which oral composing itself, and also audience intervention, constrain and enrich performance (Okpewho, *op. cit.* pp. 159–60, 194–202). See also David Abercrombie, 'A Phonetician's View of Verse Structure', in *Studies in Phonetics and Linguistics* (London: Routledge and Kegan Paul, 1965), pp. 16–25; W.K. Wimsatt (ed.) *Versification: Major Language Types* (New York: New York University, 1974); Geoffrey Leech, *A Linguistic Guide to English Poetry* (Harlow: Longman, 1969) pp. 52–125; David Crystal, 'Intonation and Metrical Theory' in *The English Tone of Voice* (London: Edward Arnold, 1975), pp. 105–24. Perry B. Yoder, in 'Biblical Hebrew', in Wimsatt (*op. cit.*), pp. 52–65, treats Hebrew parallelism as metrical, as I would hesitate to. I take 'Dirge' to be verse (composition in lines) using parallelism, but not metrical (syllable or stress-count organised).

14 The personal pronoun is closely related to what Halliday calls the interpersonal function of language. When it is the subject of a clause its position typically decides whether a statement, a question, or a command is meant. More subtle variations within these categories, such as the difference

between a command and a plea, a statement and a confession, are shown primarily through intonation. (See M.A.K. Halliday, 'Modes of Meaning and Modes of Expression' in J. Allerton, Edward Carney, David Holdcroft (eds), *Function and Context in Linguistic Analysis: essays offered to William Haas* (Cambridge: Cambridge University Press, 1979), pp. 57–79.

15 The imperative clauses such as 'Tell them', 'someone say it for us' constitute pleas; while the declarative clauses have the interpersonal force of confessions, for example, 'We have no mouths to say it with'. The intonational implication of the structures still leaves the reciter with a good deal of leeway as to actual vocal tunes to be used in performance.

16 M.A.K. Halliday and Ruqaiya Hasan, *Cohesion in English* (Harlow: Longman, 1976), p. 4. Basil Bernstein, in *Class, Codes and Control, Volume 1*, (London: Routledge and Kegan Paul, 1971), pp. 123–36, treats the question in terms of his 'restricted' and 'elaborated' codes, which Walter Ong regards as finally based on the difference between oral and written. See Ong, *Literacy and Orality* (London: Methuen, 1982), p. 106. The 'dummy' or 'false' kind of reference is discussed by Halliday and Hasan, *op. cit.*, p. 298.

17 The song, in fact, will most likely show verbal variations with each performance, while all the printed copies will be identical.

18 Kofi Awoonor, *This Earth, My Brother* (London: Heinemann, 1972), p. 144.

19 *Ibid.* p. 163.

20 Kofi Awoonor, in Karen L. Morell (ed.), *In Person: Achebe, Awoonor and Soyinka at the University of Washington* (Seattle: Inst. for Comparative and Foreign Area Studies, University of Washington, 1975), p. 141.

21 *Ibid.* p. 152.

22 Carl Jung, *The Spirit of Man, Art, and Literature* (London: Routledge and Kegan Paul, 1953), pp. 82–3, emphasis added.

23 The discussion takes a more explicitly Althusserian turn here, in insisting on the active role of the reader and the significant position and the influence of 'ideological state apparatuses'. See Althusser, *Lenin and Philosophy* (London: New Left Books, 1971) pp. 121–73.

24 See Ong, *op. cit.*, p. 181.

25 Althusser, *op. cit.*, p. 148.

26 Althusser, *ibid.*, pp. 121–73.

27 Solomon Iyasere, 'Criticism as Performance: A Ritual', in Eldred Jones (ed.), *African Literature Today, No. 11)* (London: Heinemann, 1980), pp. 169–74.

28 The change in the type of discourse and the discourse roles, invites comparison with the difference between the 'Yoruba' and 'British' discourse-positions in the reading of Soyinka's 'Post Mortem' in Chapter 1. In both this poem and 'Dirge' the grammatical form and vocabulary are capable of differing interpretations at the level of discourse.

29 Ong, *op. cit.*, pp. 178–9.

CHAPTER 5

Kunene's 'Shaka' and the Idea of the Poet as Teacher

Introduction

In an essay published a year after the English version of *Emperor Shaka the Great*, Mazisi Kunene writes that:

> Classical African literature takes it as its primary stategy to broaden the base of the characters through mythification and symbolism.[1]

As he says in the poem itself,

> Indeed, artists embellish their past to inspire their children.[2]

What I want to look at is the trend of this mythification and embellishment. In doing this I shall not make any claims as to the capacity of a poem to change people's attitudes or actions, nor will I deal with the ways in which a poem, as opposed to some other genre, might achieve such a goal. These are very vexed questions, neither of which has been tackled by African critics, even those who emphasise the traditional African artist's role of teacher. All I can claim is that if literature can have any bearing on political or social circumstances it is likely to be at times of crisis, such as we see now in Kunene's country, when people can be expected to reflect on the meaning of what they are doing and suffering. Yet we have to remember that what readers (or hearers) take from a work of art is affected by the attitudes they bring to it, and the social structures within which it is experienced – the school, the political party, exile, and so on. I will attempt, at the end of this account, to *relate* the implied 'teaching' of Kunene's poem to present events, but I cannot pretend to *comment*, since I do not have anything like sufficient knowledge, nor indeed sufficient experience. Nonetheless I have not been able to hide a bias towards the more radically socialist wing of the ANC.

In what ways, then, if any, might 'Emperor Shaka the Great' 'inspire' its 'children', many of whom – literally 'children' – are already practically enmeshed in political praxis, hence in political education? Kunene himself believes that poetry should not concern itself with immediate protest, but with 'long-term national and social goals'.[3] It should, in other words, set the immediate in a wider perspective, in relation to traditional Zulu, and African, values, and in relation to the Ancestors, one of whom is Shaka himself.

In looking at Kunene's interpretation of, and mythification of, Shaka, I will divide my account into two parts, an artificial division because the two parts overlap a good deal. First I want to look at Shaka as an embodiment of a model Zulu or African leader, the public and political Shaka; then I want to say something about Kunene's study of Shaka's mind, Shaka the rejected child, the vulnerable mystic.

Shaka as Model Leader

Following the practice, as he sees it, of 'classical African literature', Kunene presents a systematically slanted view of his protagonist. It is an 'Africanist' interpretation, as Slater[4] has forcefully noted in his attack on the historiographical outlook of the poem. Kunene highlights Shaka's individual genius, and wherever he can, he denies accusations of brutality and bloodthirstiness made by earlier commentators, or he deflects them so that Shaka's role is less blameworthy than has usually been assumed.

Thus he denies that Shaka was illegitimate, that he had any hand in the capture and killing of his mentor, Dingiswayo, that he put unproductive old men to death, that he was responsible for the death of his half-brother, or for the massacres that followed the death of his mother.

I will give two examples of this exculpatory trend. The first is over the alleged killing of his half-brother, Sigujana, who had been installed as his successor by Shaka's father, Senzangakhona, at least in Omer-Cooper's and other versions. Omer-Cooper writes,

> Dingiswayo, anxious to confirm his authority over the Zulu by establishing his nominee as their chief, lent Shaka a regiment and with this assistance he was able to overcome his half-brother, Sigujana, and put him to death.[5]

The commoner form of the story, which Omer-Cooper is following, has it that Senzangakhona, Shaka's natural father, was particularly anxious to keep him off the Zulu throne, and so had made Sigujana his heir. Kunene alters this. Now Sigujana is presented as a usurper, who has not been able to consolidate his position against other claimants; civil war is raging and Shaka comes to save a degenerating situation on behalf of the Zulu people. Shaka's advancing army simply comes upon the corpse of Sigujana, 'stabbed in between the shoulder blades'.[6] Shaka is absolved and his half-brother further condemned by the implication that, stabbed in the back, he was a coward and so doubly unworthy to rule.

A similar recasting of events in earlier versions occurs over the mass-killings that follow Nandi's death. Others than Shaka are blamed.

> Those who bore ancient grudges against each other
> Now seized the moment to vent their revenge
> Claiming to act in the king's name.[7]

However, there are some aspects of these horrific events that are not deflected in this way; nor is the incident in which Shaka orders a live foetus to be cut from a woman's womb. I will return to these in the next section.

Slater attacks the Africanist perspective of Kunene's poem by placing Shaka in (a Marxist analysis of) his historical position, mentioning forces other than his individual genius which would contribute to an explanation of his actions. For example, the increase in warlikeness is explained in terms of population pressure. He emphasises the 'entirely favourable image of Shaka himself' presented in the poem.

This is, to a great extent, the trend of Kunene's mythification and embellishment. But Kunene is, of course, fully aware of it. We have to understand him as showing, not an analysis of the historical Shaka, but a portrait of an ideal African ruler. Such an approach places emphasis on the character and role of such a ruler as an individual. It also makes use of traditional Zulu conceptions of kingship. Shaka is shown as being, within the court circle, sensitive to criticism, and democratic, regarding these qualities as traditional attributes of the good Zulu ruler.

> As our forefathers have told us:
> 'A ruler only rules through the people'[8]

even though the actual Shaka seems to have achieved such dominance through his control of the new army that he probably ruled much more autocratically than the dictum allows. The Zulu values shown are strikingly like those noted by Gluckman,[9] though Gluckman was careful to note that these were internalised norms, not necessarily actual practice. The democratic Shaka can be seen in the passage where Zihlandlo remonstrates with him most frankly:

...through haste you violated the authority of the Assembly.[10]

Shaka accepts the plain speaking as 'profound thoughts'[11] and although he does not finally accept the advice being offered about battle tactics, he is shown as overruling Zihlandlo on the basis of greater wisdom, and after consideration of alternatives. This is an intellectual Shaka whose decisions are presented as justified by circumstances and reflection. Kunene moves us a good way from the impatient tyrant of some traders' accounts.

Shaka is also presented as an innovating ruler, as might be expected. But here Kunene gives a new shaping to the idea of tradition. To Senzangakhona he attributes the erroneous static view of tradition by which

It is only the Ancestors who know how to guide us.[12]

No, Shaka says, we must control our own fates and make our own values.

...in human affairs there are no eternal laws;
Each generation makes a consensus of its own laws.[13]

The present is always sovereign, to be grasped; tradition is not the same as custom.

Despite this, and despite Kunene's apparently ignoring the striking movement towards militaristic values in Zulu society during Shaka's time, he assumes a basic Zulu ethic, contrasting Zulu values with those of the 'White Strangers'.

[T]o them wealth far surpasses the bonds of kinship.
From this all their obsessions originate[14]

Shaka says. This, and the reference to rival rulers in Southern Africa as 'bandits', betrays some Zulu chauvinism. But not racism. Shaka is also made to say of King: 'I often forget he is a foreigner or a white man.[15]

Another quite marked mythification is the idea that Shaka is a very popular leader, even though also much feared. With his death,

The whole Zulu army filled the region with their mourning songs.[16]

although most other accounts claim that there was no very strong reaction to Shaka's murder, in particular not from the army, which, returning from a failed mission, could expect the most severe punishment,[17] though the logic of this is implicitly questioned in Plaatje's *Mhudi*.[18] This popularity, and Shaka's democracy within the court circle, are to an extent contradicted by other passages, such as:

He knew he had few friends who would speak without fear.[19]

and

For those eager to be loved never make great rulers[20]

which reflect what must be a genuine conflict for all populist rulers.

The ruling-class perspective from which Kunene writes is shown most clearly in what he choses to describe naturalistically, and what he does not. For example, before Shaka's inauguration we are given a picturesque image of the preparations.

> Beautiful women of the land sat in the shade, braiding their hair.
> They reaped and crushed the fragrance of young scented flowers.
> They gossiped about their future in the king's household.
> Great processions gathered from all directions.
> Red feathers quivered as the heroes hurried to the royal city.[21]

The scene is complete and idyllic. There is no close focus on the labour required to gather all these flowers, nor on the real prospects of these young women as members of Shaka's seraglio – to become one of hundreds of closely watched 'sisters' with no prospect of normal family or sexual life, nor of (surviving) children. 'Their future in the king's household' leaves all this in vagueness. The incoming soldiers, too, are treated at this commentary-box distance.

By contrast, Kunene expresses very subtly and economically the tensions and readjustments of position involved in Shaka's new regime, as it affects those close to him, with Nandi now taking the place of his aunt, Mkhabayi as first lady. The tensions need not be spelt out because they are there in the situation, in the family, and known to Kunene's likely audience.

> Princess Mkhabayi silently entered the arena,
> Walking high like a cloud over the mountains.
> As she came before the king she peered deep into his eyes.
> The IziChwe regiments watched intently from their semi-circle positions.
> Princess Mkhabayi bowed low and shouted the royal salute...
> She opened her lips as if to speak
> But she only gestured to Nomchobo directing her eyes to Nandi...[22]

Here, at the level of court politics, we have the close focus of eyes meeting eyes, the unspoken readjustments in power relations, which primarily concern Kunene. But there is no view from 'below', no faint grins from the tough IziChwe soldiers at Mkhabayi's regal discomfiture, no commoners nudging each other, alert to the slightest betrayal of Mkhabayi's real feelings, a half-stumble, the quickening of the eyelashes.

Connected to this bias in focus is Kunene's treatment of battle scenes. For a martial epic 'Emperor Shaka the Great' is remarkably distant in its treatment of battle violence. Kunene never gets down to the horrors as Mofolo does, with Homeric impact.

...he smashed the skull of one of them and his little brain fell out, and he died belching like someone who had drunk too much beer. That stick, as it came up, split someone's chin apart so that his jaws were separated and his tongue dangled in space...[23]

Mofolo presents Shaka as ruthless and barbaric, and had Kunene emphasised the violence in this way, he might have risked falling in with this interpretation. But his commentary-box view of battles is, in a sense, evasive. He never attempts to portray the *tension* between Shaka's creativity and his destructiveness.

Shaka's Mind and Mysticism

Kunene's Africanist perspective may be looked at, from one point of view, as an attempt to present his subject as Shaka himself may have perceived it. We are asked to enter imaginatively into his moral and political world as, to Shaka, it actually seemed to be. In this sense Kunene is naturalistic, at the level of the consciousness of Shaka and his peers. It is not surprising, therefore, that Kunene shows a particular interest in and sympathy for Shaka the individual. We can look at his psychology from two points of view. First there is the process of his socialisation, then there is Kunene's presentation of his deeper thoughts in his maturity, the vulnerable and affective sides of his nature which have not been presented before in such detail, nor so compellingly.

We have seen how Kunene tends to clear Shaka of allegations of cruelty and the perpetration of atrocities. Sometimes he retells the story, and at others he takes an 'understanding' view, seeing a particular event in psychological rather than moral terms. This is particularly clear in his treatment of the incident in which Shaka has a foetus cut from the mother's womb. This is presented by Shaka as a punishment for the woman's infidelity, which traditionally carried the death penalty. Shaka argues that sexual infidelity threatens the stability of the nation. He dismisses the protestation of the prosecutor that 'the nation may be repulsed at such an outrageous act'[24] on the grounds that squeamishness is a form of weakness and superstition. He says,

It is through such fears people fail to execute justice.[25]

When the mutilation is done Kunene turns our attention at once from both the actual details (not described) and the moral question, and on to the moment of mystical insight it affords Shaka.

Many looked in horror at the spectacle before them
But none dared show their feelings of terror. .
Only Shaka followed with his eyes everv detail.
Finally he said: 'At last I have seen
How an infant lies in its mother's womb.'
He turned away and fell into deep thought.
He wandered off, as if obsessed by some mysterious memory.[26]

Shaka, then, goes 'beyond good and evil' in a kind of ruthless quest not really for justice, but for an insight into the fundamentals of human existence and origins. The passage reveals an intellectual kind of ruthlessness, but also vulnerability. Omer-Cooper makes the insightful suggestion that Shaka's alleged killing of his own child (which had been hidden from him by Nandi) might have a psychological basis, beyond the obvious practical consideration of eliminating future rivals.

Shaka also may have regarded a child of his as a reminder of his own mortality.[27]

The 'mysterious memory' almost certainly refers to some such awareness. Shaka's psychology is seen by Kunene in relation to the poles of birth and death, and the deepest of his emotions are connected to his early traumatic childhood. Shaka says,

You shall never know how deep are the fears of a growing boy[28]

In its main outline Kunene's biography follows the received narrative and explanation, showing Shaka as a man compensating for early insecurity and lack of identity. Vilakazi, in many ways Kunene's poetic forebear, pinpoints the central obsession of Shaka: his relation to his mother. He puts this in what now seem quite Freudian terms.

For was your mother not a marvel
Whose beauty of mind and body were unrivalled? –
Her hair alone cast on men a spell:
Thus many concubines had hair like hers.[29]

And Shaka's development does conform in a number of ways to that of Oedipus. Like Oedipus he survives his father's attempt to dispose of him as a child, and is brought up as a relative commoner in exile. He symbolically murders his father when he usurps the throne Senzangakhona had done his best to keep from him; he comes to Zululand as an outsider bringing stability, as Oedipus had to Thebes, and he installs his mother as 'mother of the nation', a position not unlike that of Jocasta, the symbolically incestuous relation – hinted at in Vilakazi's lines – being suggested by Shaka's unwillingness to take a wife, and his fear of having children. But, though some of this is implicit in Kunene's poem, he is by no means a Freudian. Yet he does stress Shaka's closeness to his mother, and to his sister. We may see, perhaps, his condemnation of sexual irregularity, together with his severe curtailment of the sexual life of men of fighting age, as a reaction to the circumstances of his own conception. In condemning the woman whose child is to be cut out of her, he says,

> Whoever succumbs to the body's simple invitations
> Violates the human laws and becomes no more than a beast.[30]

But we cannot but remember – a further aspect of Shaka's own 'mysterious memory' – the very passionate and irregular union which led to his own existence. Of Senzangakhona and Nandi's love making, Kunene writes,

> They fell together behind the growth of bushes.
> They loved as though to celebrate their final day on earth.[31]

The description is a good deal more animated here than in the passage in which the child is removed, but again Kunene links conception and death. And this succumbing to 'the body's simple invitations' certainly does threaten social stability: it produces Shaka.

The degree to which Shaka depends on his mother is revealed in the structure of the narrative. While she is alive he devotes himself to action, to living out her aspirations for him; but with her death the military and political pace of the narrative slows down, and the poem becomes much more contemplative. It is now that we see the vulnerable side of Shaka, and related to it, his capacity for deep friendship and mystical awareness – which in the form of communication with his Ancestors is also a kind of historical awareness. While Thompson summarily declares that

> success gradually went to his head and eventually undermined his sense of reality.[32]

Kunene shows him as concerned with a different dimension of reality, the reality, to him, of his dead relatives and the Ancestors. The massacres that follow the death of Nandi *are* explained in terms of a kind of loss of contact with reality, but this is seen as distraction by grief, not madness. Shaka temporarily loses his grip on political affairs and indiscipline in the state follows. Kunene again takes the 'understanding' line.

> If the death of Nandi has turned his mind
> Then it is a weakness that still attests to his greatness,
> For, truly, there is no lover who is without fault.[33]

Notice in passing, the ambiguous 'lover'.
It is only now, in its mystical form, that death unsettles Shaka.

I am obsessed with the voices of the dead.
They who were once close to me come back.
I tremble as though death had not been with me all my life.[34]

As in the passage where he has the child excised, here too, Shaka is brought face to face with the idea of his mortality. Kunene now pays a good deal of attention to his dreams.

He dreamt he saw Mbiya and his mother, Nandi.
They were absorbed in deep conversation.
Constantly they whispered to each other,
But when he came closer, they were suddenly silent.
They turned to him, staring him in the eye.[35]

The writing here is very effective, and where Kunene is verbally striking it is often over face-to-face encounters, or expressions of the face. For example, Shaka's unease at getting a message purportedly from the Ancestors is expressed as follows.

Shaka did not comment. He only stared at the ground.
His eyes were like those of a drunken man following an ant.[36]

Here, naturalistically, he focuses on Shaka as leader and man, and on his relation to the supernatural, cosmological forces which Kunene believes the poet should concentrate on. It is this area that interests him most immediately, here that his language is often at its most vital and resonantly particular.

Conclusion

I have tried to indicate that the trend of Kunene's embellishment of Shaka amounts to the exculpation of the public figure, and towards the 'understanding' of the individual. The poet writes from the perspective of the ruling family, stressing Zulu – and by extension, African – values and continuities, and, as ruling families are apt to do, emphasises nationalism. The pedagogical implication of the poem, looked at in Kunene's terms, is that it may broaden and deepen the understanding of the 'children' it is addressed to. It does not aim at philosophically simplistic comprehensibility such as Chinweizu advocates, nor proletarian immediacy such as we find in Ngugi's recent work. Yet events in

South Africa do *render* the themes of 'Emperor Shaka the Great' relevant to the immediate experience of its readers, especially the actual children who are stoning the police and being shot in the townships. The poem is in Zulu (originally) and deals with a Zulu hero, but Shaka can no longer be seen as only Zulu since, to a large extent he is now an African figure, and transcends ethnic boundaries; and Zulu is a language many non-Zulus speak. The poem has an obvious relation to the modern quest for black unity in South Africa, for organisation and martial courage, at a time when the conflict is becoming more violent, and when anti-apartheid parties are still not united, and a significant number of blacks man the armed forces and the police.

Kunene himself has been an active worker in the ANC, and also, paradoxically as it now begins to seem, an admirer of Gatsha Buthelezi, the Zulu leader who has so often attacked the ANC for its Leninist type of underground operations and consequent lack of rapport with everyday black life.[37] The poem is dedicated to Buthelezi: and indeed Buthelezi resembles Shaka in being a popular royal leader with great charisma. Kunene's Shaka does not, of course, advocate non-violence as Buthelezi has, though it may be argued that Buthelezi's position here is tactically pragmatic. Whatever contradictions we might discern in Kunene's adherence to both the ANC and to Buthelezi, it does seem that the ideological trend of 'Emperor Shaka the Great' is towards bringing the immediate struggles against apartheid under the wider sway of the Zulu ruling family, or, by extension, some form of 'top-down' populism under a charismatic 'great leader', a further 'embellishment' and 'mythification', no doubt. And this would be a 'long-term national and social goal'.

To most Africans, especially those on the left, it is an ominous and familiar scenario. Despite this, we learn from this poem. We see Shaka from a point of view which is probably very close to the image of himself with which Shaka identified. This Kunene has shown with great skill and sensitivity. His very success brings into question the didacticism which he has explicitly claimed for, and demands of, the African poet. It shows that there is always a difference between what the poet may wish to teach his readers and what they may learn from his trying to do that.[38]

NOTES

1 Mazisi Kunene, 'The Relevance of African Cosmological Systems to African Literature Today', in Eldred Jones (ed.), *African Literature Today, No 11* (London: Heinemann, 1980), p. 200.
2 Mazisi Kunene, *Emperor Shaka the Great* (London: Heinemann, 1979), p. 166.
3 Kunene, 1980, p. 191.

4   Henry Slater, 'Shaka Zulu, Apartheid and the Politics of the Liberation of Historiography of South Africa', a paper presented to the Fifth SAUSSC Conference, 1982.
5   J.D. Omer-Cooper, *Zulu Aftermath* (London: Longman, 1966), p. 30.
6   *Ibid.* p. 70.
7   *Emperor Shaka the Great*, p. 337.
8   *Ibid.* p. 163.
9   M. Gluckman, 'The Kingdom of the Zulu in South Africa' in M. Fortes and E. Evans-Pritchard (eds), *African Political Systems* (London: Oxford Univ. Press, 1940), pp. 23–55.
10 *Emperor Shaka the Great*, p. 375.
11 *Ibid.* p. 376.
12 *Ibid.* p. 34.
13 *Ibid.* p. 55.
14 *Ibid.* p. 296.
15 *Ibid.* p. 407.
16 *Ibid.* p. 427.
17 *Zulu Aftermath* p. 42; Peter Becker, *Rule of Fear* (Harmondsworth: Penguin, 1964); Leonard Thompson, 'Co-operation and Conflict: the Zulu Kingdom and Natal' in Leonard Thompson and Monica Wilson (eds), *The Oxford History of South Africa, Volume 1* (London: Oxford University Press, 1969), p. 334–90.
18 Sol Plaatje, *Mhudi* (Johannesburg: Quagga Press, 1975), p. 129.
19 *Emperor Shaka the Great*, p. 276.
20 *Ibid.* p. 251.
21 *Ibid.* p. 78.
22 *Ibid.* pp. 78–9.
23 Thomas Mofolo, *Chaka* (London: Heinemann, 1981), p. 32.
24 *Emperor Shaka the Great*, p. 194.
25 *Ibid.* p. 194.
26 *Ibid.* p. 195.
27 *Zulu Aftermath*, p. 35.
28 *Emperor Shaka the Great*, p. 76.
29 B.W. Vilakazi, *Zulu Horizons* (Johannesburg: Witwatersrand University Press, 1973), p. 36.
30 *Emperor Shaka the Great*, p. 194.
31 *Ibid.* p. 7.
32 'Co-operation and Conflict: the Zulu Kingdom and Natal', p. 350 (see note 17 above).
33 *Emperor Shaka the Great*, p. 342.
34 *Ibid.* p. 379.
35 *Ibid.* p. 422.
36 *Ibid.* p. 257.
37 Oscar Dhlomo, 'The Strategy of Inkatha and its Critics' in *Journal of Asian and African Studies*, XVIII, 1–2, 1983, p. 52.
38 I am grateful to colleagues Mbulelo Mzamane and Bala Ushman for criticisms of this essay at the draft stage.

CHAPTER 6

'The Actual Dialogue': Discourse, Form and Performance

A poem can be described as a modified conversational 'turn'.[1] The poet takes the role of utterer, and the reader that of responder. The commentator articulates and explicates the responses of the reader as the latter follows through the unfolding of the poem in time. The conversational model may be defended on theoretical grounds as the basis of a materialist poetic,[2] but in the following commentary on Mongane Walle Serote's poem, 'The Actual Dialogue', it will be used primarily to highlight a conception of commentary which brings out the dynamic and interactive features of poetic discourse. Commentary is taken to be a 'running commentary' in retrospect of the reader's view of the close twists and turns of the poet's text.

A poem is not the same as a conversational turn; the most important difference is that in the exchange of a poem, even if this occurs face-to-face in a live performance, there are conventions to be observed, different from those in conversations.[3] The most important of these is the attention that must be given to the linguistic medium as such and *its* meanings as well as the poet's.

The kind of commentary such a model suggests is more impersonal in some ways than conventional literary criticism, since it uses concepts and methods drawn from linguistics and semiotics. On the other hand it allows for greater subjectivity by the commentator in giving his actual associations as they occur, and relating the text to his everyday life. Such associations, however, can themselves be made articulate, and related to aspects of the commentator's background and ideological position, his development as a 'subject'.[4] This dimension of the commentary has been curtailed, since my own particular perspectives on the poem in relation to everyday praxis are so untypical as to be of limited interest to students of African poetry. They will be evident to the watchful reader in the overall construction of this essay, and in particular in the comments about the conception of textual unity and elegance on pages 72–4.

The model implies a relativist position in the sense that critical approval amounts to wanting to go on with the reading, being able to sustain the reader's role; while rejection is shown in a reader's growing sense of inability to sustain the role, or just getting bored.

THE ACTUAL DIALOGUE

Do not fear, Baas.	1
It's just that I appeared	2
And our faces met	3
In this black night that's like me	4
Do not fear –	5
We will always meet	6
When you do not expect me.	7
I will appear,	8
In the night that's black like me.	9
Do not fear –	10
Blame your heart	11
When you fear me –	12
I will blame my mind	13
When I fear you	14
In the night that's black like me.	15
Do not fear, Baas,	16
My heart is vast as the sea	17
And your mind as the earth.	18
It's awright, baas,	19
Do not fear.[5]	20

The poem itself represents a conversation, or a turn in one, in which the black alone speaks. This conversation within the poem, in an 'imaginary situation'[6] must be distinguished from the exchange between the poet and the reader in a 'practical situation'. It is this latter which is being compared to a conversational turn, even though the situation is attenuated by the separation of the times of composition and reading, and the geographical positions of composer and reader.

Commentary

The titles of poems are often obscure in the sense that they cannot be fully interpreted at a first reading until the whole text has been understood. The title has to be 'reglossed'[7] when the nature of the 'Actual Dialogue' has been described.

The text begins with what Burton calls an 'opening move',[8] in which the black both announces himself to the white, and lets the reader know that it is a white he is addressing, by his use of the word 'Baas'. He moves on to a 'supporting' move in which he informs the baas about his own blackness. But the lines

It's just that I appeared
And our faces met

are not strictly necessary in the imaginary situation. The baas can see that the man has appeared. The lines are included primarily for the poet to inform the reader what is happening. Also, it is odd for the black to refer to his own blackness in the way he does in line 4. From the point of view of the practical discourse this 'informative' act has a point: letting the reader know that it is night; but from the point of view of the imaginary situation it is superfluous. However, there are occasions when stating the obvious has a point. One of these is to influence the listener to see something *more* than the obvious. The black wants to make the baas ponder the self-evident situation the two of them suddenly find themselves in. He seems to want to *draw attention to* the baas's fear, and to his own blackness. In comparing his colour to the blackness of the night he uses a cliché common to many cultures, that blackness is fearful and symbolises evil. This symbolism is not unique to English, but acquires an added layer of meaning in the imaginary context. The speaker seems to mention his colour in a pointed way as if to say, 'Look how black I really am!', alluding to the preoccupations in the baas's mind, showing him that the black can perceive these deep-seated anxieties. His overt reassurance, that the baas should not fear, reveals that he perceives the fear instantly, and his allusion to his blackness shows that he knows it will be the first thing to strike the baas. His capacity to insinuate himself into the baas's mind is unnerving rather than reassuring; it may conceal an intention to *foster* anxiety. Also, the black's adoption of the speech role of reassurer places him in the dominant position in the conversation. He usurps the position usually held by the white, while still using the demeaning term, 'Baas'.

Emphasising discourse in the sense in which the term is being used[9] amounts to emphasising speech. The printed form of the poem is being regarded as a script which has yet to be performed, produced like a drama. Although the script is not at all the same as the grammatical form of the text, it does tend to draw attention to form, since form is also potential in this way, awaiting, as it were, the allocation of meaning. There is a contrast between the typical meaning of the utterance, 'Do not fear, Baas' and an untypical one.[10] The contrast is *between* interpretations at the level of discourse, between interpreting the utterance interactionally as a reassurance or as menace.

The meaning of 'menace' is not simply imposed. It is present in the presupposition behind the utterance. If the speaker tells the baas not to fear, he presupposes that at the time of utterance the baas is afraid; and he also implies that he himself is not afraid. While he is reassuring the baas by advising him to *stop* fearing, he is also drawing attention to the fact that now he *is* afraid. He has, after all, made the topic of the white's fear the content of his opening remark and the use of the negative still pinpoints that topic. The way presupposition is highlighted (on this interpretation) can be shown from possible intonation. If the black were giving the white a simple reassurance he would probably use a falling intonation like this:

```
DO not   F
             E
                A
                   R
                     b
                       a
                         a
                           s
```

The capitals indicate relatively prominent or stressed syllables. But if the black wanted to draw attention to something presupposed he would probably make use of the fall-rise tone, which usually carries the general meaning of 'what we have already mentioned, or what we both already understand to be so'. This can be illustrated as follows:

```
DO not F   R      B   S
          E          A
            A          A
```

or perhaps:

```
                              s
                              a
                              a
        DO not F   R      b
                E
                A
```

When an actual intonation is used by a performer he commits himself to a particular interpretation. And even in silent reading a reader tends to assume or 'hear' typical tunes which are modified as different interpretations are entertained. It is in this sense that the silent reader is a potential performer.

So far the reader has been represented as the silent partner in the discourse, responding cooperatively by looking into the ramifications of the poet's text, assuming that is what he expects. This has focused attention on the metaphorical thrust of the black's discourse in the imaginary situation, how he unnerves the white by usurping his position as 'baas' and putting himself in touch with typical, and imagined, 'white' thought-processes. The identification continues in the next lines, as is suggested by the choice of the word 'appeared'. It presumes the viewpoint of the baas, since it is to him that the speaker appears. The word is not supported by a locative phrase such as 'from the garden', and is untypical in being used in the first person like this. Although 'I' takes the position of grammatical subject, it has a passive sense, presupposing that some other person has the role of observer. That is, it is closer to meaning 'I was seen' than to 'I saw'. The sudden appearance of the black suggests an 'apparition', a ghost, again typically associated with night, and beyond that the shadow-like presence of the black which haunts all aspects of white South African life, and may be connected with the fear of death. Talking about the fear of death in more general terms, McCarthy writes,

> The typical course of death-anxiety in childhood dreams and fantasies starts with the terror of animals and monsters and progresses to part-animal, part-human monsters, to robbers, ghosts and burglars.[11]

It is easy to see how such a pattern might be assimilated into a racist society, the actual fear of the black burglar or intruder being potent among middle-class whites as a threat to life and also to an entire way of life. The apparition may be seen as a creation of the white's own fantasy, his own unconscious addressing him, his own 'soul' in the form of the black.[12] However, on balance, it seems more likely that the interpenetration of the two characters is slightly different, that they are separate and that as it goes on, the black's insinuation into the white's mind tends to be on the white's own terms.

In line 4 the black, again informing the reader rather than the baas, compares himself to the blackness of the night. The fact that 'I' has already just been mentioned means that the most likely intonation will be one in which 'me' is not stressed, for example,

$$
\text{in the NIGHT that's BLACK} \quad \text{L} \atop \text{I} \atop \text{K} \atop \text{E} \quad \text{me}
$$

as against the citational

$$
\text{in the NIGHT that's BLACK like} \quad \text{M} \atop \text{E}
$$

that is, the pattern most likely to be 'heard' in the mind if the words are met out of context. Yet a speaker might in fact adopt this citational intonation if he aimed to *convey* the sense of citation. After all he is looking at himself, again, from the baas's viewpoint and he is citing the way in which whites speak about blacks. So if he were to speak this in a citational or quoting tone of voice the mocking posture we have already detected would be extended. Again a structure which would be most typically interpreted, out of any particular context, as self-derogation, is given the untypical force of self-assertion and mocking menace. This is a variation on the posture adopted by Césaire in defiantly playing out the role allocated to him by white prejudice.

Serote goes on manipulating discourse-roles in the next lines where he shifts from the immediate past and present to the future.

We will always meet
When you do not expect me

which on one interpretation is a forecast as to fact, but on another a threat that the white's peace of mind is going to be shaken continuously in the future. The white will not succeed in shutting the black out of consciousness.

The 'negritudinal' theme is taken up again in line 11 in which Serote opens up a subtopic (or 'bound opening' in Burton's terminology) about the supposed differences between white and black racial characters. The view also figures in some black consciousness texts. The idea is that the black and white differ in the way the 'mind' and the 'heart' differ. The white's approach to life is rationalistic and involves repression of emotional spontaneity, generosity and communalism in favour of thrift, self-control and other bourgeois values. The values and character traits which the white represses and regards as vices and threats to his success in life are the very ones which the black rejoices in. Looked at as a description of urban western society there is obviously something in the repression hypothesis, and this has been convincingly related to racism. Describing an aspect of Neumann's work, Manganyi writes,

> The unconscious becomes, under conditions governing the old ethic, the repository of all the bodily appetites that were rejected by society. It is this rejected portion of the individual and social existence which creates tensions not only in the individual but also in the life of whole groups and nations. The tensions which arise from this massive collective repression are resolved through the process of projection which, in the case of the collective, sometimes leads to scapegoating.[13]

The supposed black character is unrepressed, generous, at home with his body and sexuality and generally intuitive. Where the white is all mind, the black is all heart. While there is an element of truth in this, it seriously oversimplifies, and beyond that tilts the balance of the comparison against the black, though this may not be immediately obvious. While the traits of the black are those which the white has repressed as the price for economic development, it can hardly be claimed that the white traits have been 'rejected' by the black. If the black's character is indeed like this, as part of his nature and culture then he is always going to be dominated by the better-organised and better-armed white baas, a perpetual natural Caliban manipulated by an artful Prospero. Furthermore, the whole idea of allocating racial characters is based on an emphasis on racial (and tribal) differences, which make the Bantustan policy possible. The qualities of spontaneity and intuitiveness alleged to belong with the black character are much better looked upon as the result of social and political conditioning. Spontaneity is commonly regarded as a lovable quality in children, and intuition a characteristic of women, groups who both need to be controlled and restricted 'for their own good'.

This poem was composed at a time when Serote was beginning to be affected by the ideas of the Black Consciousness Movement in which emphasis on racial differences, albeit as a tactical political move, may have given the contrast between white mind and black heart an added currency. Hence it is difficult to be sure whether Serote himself wants his reader to take the idea seriously or not, or perhaps as the serious conviction of the black character he is portraying in the poem. Mzamane does not discuss these particular lines in any detail, but his conception of the poem as a whole suggests that he takes the black to be speaking in a much more straightforward way than my reading allows.[14] He sets the poem in its political context and claims that Serote is putting forward the idea that the 'actual dialogue' should be between black and white and not between white and other whites outside South Africa. He takes the poem to be a plea by Serote for political understanding between the races, and an identification of fear as the obstacle preventing this. Throughout his career, Serote has vacillated between his anger at white dominance and his desire for reconciliation and healing the wounds. The interpretation put forward here, which resembles the interpretation Mzamane gives to 'They Do It' – that is, a rejection of the white liberal position – may, however, also be seen as a dramatising of Serote's vacillation between reconciliation and aggression, since the poem certainly expresses both attitudes: reconciliation in its ideational content, and aggression as its interpersonal attitude.

This interpretation is preferred because it makes the poem more interesting, as *making use* of post-negritude clichés rather than allowing them to usurp the black's mind. However, if Mzamane is right, and the poem is intended as a straightforward expression of reassurance, it may be argued that the poem can be made to go deeper than Serote himself does, at a philosophical level. We may see it as a partly-conscious expression of Serote's own vacillation.

If the opposition between black heart and white mind is taken as a yet further citation of a typical white liberal position, which has been assimilated by the black, then the tension between typical and non-typical discourse acts is maintained in this part of the text. The black continues to present himself to the white in the white's own image of him, in the white's own clichés of black generosity of nature, an image to be found in *Othello* and before, as well as Césaire. And *it is this image of the black* that the white need not fear. The ironical citation of it, however, undermines it, and so threatens the white.

Serote is a verbally inventive writer and the appearance of these clichés therefore suggests citation rather than lazy writing. The words 'heart' and 'mind' are, after all, very tired symbols for attitudes, and the geographical images of the sea and the earth, at least as used here, particularly lifeless, even though Serote's poems often make use of sea and river imagery.

In line 11, the act of threatening reassurance is replaced by one of advising.

Blame your heart
When you fear me –

The fear he sees in the white's face is to be *blamed on* his heart, that is on his atrophied spontaneity, where he is inadequate compared to the black. His incapacity to go out to the other man causes his fear. This explains the white's fear of the black only up to a point. His reserved nature has been instilled in him from an early age, and culturally, over centuries. The fear he has of the black is psychological in its immediate expression, but also it is economic. The ghostly shadow-figure of the black 'monster' which is all passion and no mind is also evoked as an ideological image to justify his repression of the black. Since the image of the black corresponds to the repressed urges in his own unconscious, his 'heart', blaming his 'heart' comes to much the same as blaming the black himself, or rather the image he has of the black.

But in what way is the black himself to blame *his* fear of the white on his own 'mind'? This is not repressed, though it may be argued that the black has been 'deprived of his mind' by white ideology and dominance, in the sense that he has been allowed no scope to control his own fate or seriously develop his education. But it is difficult to see how he is responsible for this, hence how he should *blame* his mind. His fear of the white is well motivated and entirely rational (as the white's fear of him is not, or not wholly). He has good reason to fear imprisonment, police attack, and that in the imaginary situation represented in the poem, the white will raise the alarm or produce a gun. The only reason he might blame his own mind is if he accepts the view that there *is* something in his racial character, not shaped by the white's domination, that makes that white the equivalent of the black's mind. But this, symmetrical with the idea of the white's black 'soul', is a view favourable to the white, easily assimilable to apartheid ideology. The black, then, is still citing, mimicking the advice on racial harmony which would be typical of the more progressive whites.

In line 16 the intruder reiterates his injunction against fear, and then the stereotypes of heart and mind are exchanged for the stereotypes of the sea and the earth. The black's heart is vast as is the sea, and the white's is like the earth. Yet it is not immediately clear what relation the reader is to see between the earth and the mind, and the sea and the heart. The sea is often related to human emotions, its waves, currents, tides, tempests, and so on. The earth, by contrast is solid and fixed and can be built upon and mined. At present the white does indeed control most of the earth. The earth and the sea, however, are mutually exclusive; they do not meet; they are always apart and segregated. The racially biased and based images continue, though now perhaps rather unnecessarily, since the basic point has already been forcefully enough made. The comparisons are puzzling in another way too. Why the emphasis on scale and vastness? Perhaps the black means that his capacity for sympathy is inexhaustible; but since the white's mind is 'as the earth' what can the cause be for his fear? This may be yet another layer of mockery, then?

The poem ends with a modification of the reiterated 'reopening move' which begins with the 'informative' act, 'It's awright', followed by a 'supporting move' enjoining the 'baas', now with a small 'b' not to fear. The small 'b'[15] and the colloquial 'awright' suggest the black's own dialect, not citation any longer. They indicate a more relaxed tenor, at least on the black's side, as if he may now actually 'mean what he says'. The end of a poem is the place where the cohesion of the text is usually highlighted by some kind of punchline which clinches it (here it is unlike casual conversation). Is the shift in tenor here some kind of clinching? The black may now feel genuinely sorry for the white, but this seems unlikely in view of his behaviour so far, in which he enters the white's position and witholds any kind of sympathy. More likely the black's greater intimacy means greater contempt; he has unnerved the white to the extent that now he can speak dismissively to him; his mockery becomes more relaxed as he senses his own domination of the man-to-man situation. Or, alternatively he may now be actually telling the white he need not fear *the menace and threats which have been expressed in the text so far*, through apparent reassurances.

How far is this interpretation Serote's? What if it turns out to be a creation of this reader/commentator? How far is the interpretation just an attempt on the part of the reader to retain his enthusiasm and interest in the poem, to continue to play his 'conversational' role?

It could be claimed, simply, that Serote's poem lacks development. For example, it requires almost no reglossing; that is, that the reader must reassess what he has already read and reinterpret particular words or structures retrospectively as he moves through the text, and especially when he comes to the clinching punchlines at the end. A conveniently compact example of reglossing in a whole poem can be seen in this text by the Palestinean poet, al-Qasim.

TRAVEL TICKETS

On the day you kill me	1
You'll find in my pocket	2
Travel tickets	3
To peace,	4
To the fields and the rain,	5
To people's conscience.	6
Don't waste the tickets.[16]	7

When the reader reaches line 4 he is forced to reinterpret the words 'travel tickets'. In line 3 they meant what the words typically mean, but lines 4 to 6 make him reinterpret them as 'the speaker's political values and goals', or something equivalent to that. Then, at the end of the poem, the reader's previous interpretations are upset again, since suddenly the speaker turns to ask his own murderers not to 'waste the tickets' – which means that everything that has gone before now has to be reassessed, since the reader will have assumed that the people who are to kill the speaker are his enemies and *not* interested in peace or the people's conscience, as he is.

On a 'straight' interpretation of the poem, Serote's text is not like this. The cohesion is based upon reiteration of the same or similar words, which do *not* alter their senses retrospectively. It is not necessary to 'read backwards' except in one case, the interpretation of the title. But even here 'the actual dialogue' does not take on any striking new meaning from what the words might have suggested. The text is still a little clumsy even on the interpretation that has been suggested, but this interpretation does require some reglossing, again of the title, and of the text as a whole before the final 'awright, baas', which underlines the idea that it's this particular kind of threat and understanding of him by the black, that the white needs to fear, though not this utterance of them.

The word 'dialogue' is to be reglossed in the sense that, on the interpretation offered here, the *actual* dialogue goes on below the surface (ideational) meanings of the words being exchanged. The actual dialogue is the threat – or perhaps threats – implicit in the liberal notion of 'dialogue'. The white notion of reconciliation embodied in the post-negritude clichés is a hidden threat to black self-determination, and the black's injunction not to fear is denied by the circumstances in which he articulates it (he has suddenly appeared like a burglar in the night) and in the tone of voice he uses.

From the point of view of the poet's technique, it must be admitted that this strong impact is made in the first few lines of the poem and is not decisively added to in what follows, except that at the end the change in dialect to *fanakolo* ('vernacular' or South African black dialect) does underline an aspect of the interpersonal force of the poem, being the black's sudden relaxation of threat and tension. But, although the interpretation put forward does allow interesting reglossing of the title, of the ideas of what the real status of the 'dialogue' is, the doubt that the poem lacks development, cumulation, remains.

It may, however, be objected that looking into Serote's text for this kind of cumulative textual elegance amounts to imposing western, or at least non-African, assumptions about poetic discourse. Not only African commentators have objected that the notion of strict thematic unity in a poem is distinctively western European. Writing about pre-Renaissance Welsh poetry, Gwyn Williams says,

> English and most Western European creative activity has been con-
> ditioned by the inheritance from Greece and Rome of the notion of a
> central point of interest in a poem, picture or a play, a nodal region to
> which everything leads and upon which everything depends. The
> dispersed nature of the thematic splintering of Welsh poetry is not due
> to a failure to follow this classical convention. Aneirin, Gwalchmai,
> Cynddelw and Hywel ab Owain were not trying to write poems that
> would read like Greek temples or even Gothic cathedrals but, rather
> like stone circles or the contour-following rings of the forest from which
> they fought, with hidden ways slipping from one ring to another.[17]

The limitation suggested in Serote's poem is not that it 'rambles' but that it is uneconomical. But that is the obverse of the same allegedly western cultural coin.

The way of looking at poetic textuality through analogy to other aspects of the culture concerned is instructive. Possibly features of South African society can be adduced to place against Serote's text, an obvious can-didate being the reiterative tendency of oral poetry, or in jazz, both of which inform Serote's poetry. As does the notion of poetry as drama.[18]

   While it may be legitimate to cast about in the mind to discover what Serote might have meant, whether the interpretation that comes to me, western-orientated as it may be, of Serote's concluding move into the causal tenor marked by 'awright' is acceptable, when I perform the poem the restraint of the text relaxes. For reasons not at all clear, the idea of a performer's reinterpreting a dramatic text is more acceptable than the idea of a commentator reinterpreting a poem. Yet what is the difference between an actor's making the text his own, and the literary critic's? The intonation of the performer, together with his bodily and facial acting, constitute an interpretation of the text in which the interpreter places himself in the position of the poet, or his character(s) in an imaginary situation and 'completes' the text. The restraint upon the performer is whether the words in the script, as the written form of the text now becomes, can be made to bear the intonational meanings he wants to make them bear. Clearly, a good actor may perform 'The Actual Dialogue' in the menacing and mocking-imitating way suggested above as commentator – a role now perhaps transposed to the director. In this context, again for reasons that are not clear, an audience is less likely to complain if an actor renders a text interesting, than an academic reader is if a commentator reads an inventive interpretation into it.

The discourse-role of the performing actor is not equivalent to the reader's since the performer himself addresses an audience whose own position is like that of a reader; but the member of an audience at a performance has less scope for interpretation, since an intonational and gestural layer of interpretation will be added for him by the actor; on the other hand the presence of the audience is essential to the performance, and the role of encouraging and responsive listener (comparable to the passive conversant) has much more scope, and much more influence on the playing of the actor who, in one sense, stands in the communicational shoes of the poet, if indeed he is not the poet himself. In some traditional performances the role of the audience flows over into the performer's, and the distinction between creator/performer and listener/reactor blurs, and the roles may be reversed.[19]

An actor may alter the linguistic form (grammar and vocabulary)[20] of a play or a poem to be performed. In the context of drama less constraint is usually felt than in the context of the printed page. Yet there is no reason why I should not rewrite Serote's poem in a way that pleases me better. If the impulse does come upon a reader to recast a poem the recasting he does is, surely, equivalent to the reshaping which the member of an audience in a traditional performance does, when he tells the singer to sit down and listen to how the song really should be sung – or indeed, worded. His action in doing this need not by any means be aggressive or humiliating to the original singer. It constitutes part of the whole communication, which includes communication about the ways in which the text is generated and produced. The assumption that the written word is the fixed word has its place in scholarship, but in the verbal arts it is out of place.

The focus of this essay has been on the conversation-like role of the reader. The reader becomes a commentator, or 'critic', when he articulates his reading process, such as it is, in explicit terms by producing a parallel prose text such as the present one. He becomes a performer when he uses this account, or his intuitions about the texts which might have been made explicit as a commentary, to act the poem, providing it with a realisation as speech sound.

The main difference between commenting and criticising is that commentary, while being more linguistically self-conscious and analytical in some ways, is more subjective in others, and concerned with judgement only implicitly. The commentator, like the reader, tries to play his role of filling out the meaning of the poem, seeing his own experience in it; but occasions occur when he finds himself unable to sustain the role. He has to make allowances, he doubts whether the poet really knew what he was up to, and so on. At this point he has the choice of either throwing the book down and so *de facto* dismissing the poem from con-sideration, or of enlarging his own imaginative contribution so as to make something of the poem. And if he succeeds in this he may then wonder whether the poet did not, in fact, have such an interpretation in mind all along. Who has done what becomes difficult to settle, if indeed it is needful to settle at all.

Poems are obviously not the same as conversations. Conversation as a 'base' is simply a useful yardstick and partially contrastive model. The poem that has been discussed is itself conducive to this treatment because it contains a one-sided conversation. My response is also affected by the fact that the character addressed in this conversation is white. But, in principle, the same process of reading and commentary could have been used had the poem been narrative. Using the model of discourse analysis, albeit impressionistically, focuses attention on the interactive force of the communication, what it is the poet and his reader are doing in uttering and responding, by means of the text. A similar kind of analogy, again to conversation, was made by Brecht in an explanation of his view of acting, which he compared to the demonstrative kind of relation of an anecdote as part of a turn in a conversation.[21] Discourse analysis in recent deve-lopments of systemic theory pays attention to the way in which one turn in a conversation is connected to the next, the way in which the conversation progresses through time. Using it as a model encourages the perception of a poem as a process moving through time, as in performance, and commentary as the following-through of this process, as a 'melody' of successive verbal deeds and gestures, beckoning to the reader to share the poet's movements of thought, ultimately as an example of linguistic perception as such.

The fact that the poet is inaccessible, or dead,[22] need not affect this communication; nor need the perception that I can never be sure that my interpretation corresponds to his intentions make me doubt the reality of the poet, or that he did have intentions. I need not accept what I judge to be his own interpretation. I am free to do as I would in a face-to-face conversation, to interpret his words in relation to how I respond to, assess, interpret, him, and in relation to my own interests. Self-deceptions and misconceptions pursue poets and their readers at every step, but poets and their readers are not privileged in this. Anyone with whom we interact we have to create imaginatively from our own resources of ideology, character and experience; and we each misrecognise and misidentify with the other in ways shaped by our pasts. The poet is just another other, or rather an exemplary other, since it is the very impulse towards intimacy, the sharing of his 'grain of thought'[23] which raises all these questions about the possibility of communication. The medium of intimacy, like the medium of humanity – language – is not itself intimate.

Appendix to Chapter 6
'The Actual Dialogue': Discourse Analysis

Note

Words in capitals or in italics are drawn from Burton's analysis. Words with initial capitals are taken from Halliday's discussion[24] of clause-complex relations and added to the scheme. A summary of the terms taken from Burton and Halliday is given below. Additional impressionistic comments are self-explanatory.

EXCHANGE: A unit of conversation defined by topic. The poem consists of one exchange only, so the term is not put into the analysis. It might be argued that the title consisted of a preliminary kind of exchange.

MOVE: Moves of different types make up an exchange.

OPENING MOVE is self-explanatory. It starts things off.

SUPPORTING MOVE keeps the text moving in the same drift set by the opening move.

CHALLENGING MOVE alters the drift of the text by contradicting, questioning, refusing to respond, and so on. Not necessarily aggressive.

REOPENING MOVE brings the text back to the topic being discussed before the challenge, or from a sub-topic.

BOUND OPENING MOVE opens up a sub-topic related to the exchange topic as set by the opening move.

ACT: Act 'realises' move in different ways. It is the lowest category in the 'rank scale' which includes Exchange and Move higher up. There are a large number of acts identified by Burton. Only those needed to describe the poem are listed.

DIRECTIVE enjoins some non-linguistic response.

SUMMONS draws the hearer's attention to his being addressed.

INFORMATIVE gives information.

In the 'Act' column additional terms drawn from Halliday occur:

ELABORATION clarifies by repeating in the same or different words, or exemplifying

EXTENSION develops by adding new logically related information

ENHANCEMENT provides circumstantial information

'The Actual Dialogue': Discourse Structure

MOVE	ACT	Overt	Covert	TEXT
OPENING	*directive*	reassurance	menace	1 Do not fear
	summons			Baas
SUPPORTING	*informative*	to baas	to reader	2 It's just that I appeared
	elaboration			3 And our faces met
	enhancement	description	citation	4 In this black night that's black like me
REOPENING	*directive*	reiterated reassurance	reiterated menace	5 Do not fear –
SUPPORTING	*informative*	prediction	threat	6 We will always meet
	enhancement			7 When you do not expect me.
	elaboration			8 I will appear
	enhancement	reiterated description	reiterated citation	9 In the night that's black like me
REOPENING	*directive*	reiterated reassurance	reiterated menace	10 Do not fear –
BOUND	extension	advice	citation	11 Blame your heart
OPENING	enhancement			12 When you fear me –
	informative enhancement	promise	citation	13 I will blame my mind
	enhancement			14 When I fear you
	enhancement	description		15 In the night that's black like me
REOPENING	*directive* summons	reiterated	reiterated	16 Do not fear Baas
BOUND	*informative*	advice	citation	17 My heart is vast as the sea
OPENING	extension			18 And your mind as the earth
REOPENING	*informative* summons	reassurance	dismissal	19 It's awright baas
SUPPORTING	*directive*	reiterated reassurance	reassurance about covert menace	20 Do not fear.

NOTES

1   The term 'turn' is drawn from systemic functional discourse analysis, as developed by J. McH. Sinclair and R.M. Coulthard, *Towards an Analysis of Discourse* (London: Oxford University Press, 1973); Malcolm Coulthard and Martin Montgomery (eds) *Studies in Discourse Analysis* (London: Routledge and Kegan Paul, 1981); Ronald Carter and Deirdre Burton (eds) *Literary Text and Language Study* (London: Edward Arnold, 1982). See Chapter 1.

2   Mary Louise Pratt, *Towards a Speech Act Theory of Literary Discourse* (Bloomington: Indiana University Press, 1977).

3   For a fuller exposition of this view of poetry see Chapter 1.

4 This concept of the 'subject' is taken from Lacan. See Rosalind Coward and John Ellis, *Language and Materialism* (London: Routledge and Kegan Paul, 1977), particularly Chapter 6, 'On the Subject of Lacan', pp. 93–121; also *The Four Fundamental Concepts of Psycho-Analysis* by Jaques Lacan, edited by Jacques-Alain Miller, and translated by Alan Sheridan (Harmondsworth: Penguin, 1977); Jacques Lacan: *Ecrits: A Selection*, translated by Alan Sheridan London: Tavistock Publications, 1977). See Glossary.

5 Robert Royston (ed.) *Black Poets in South Africa* (London: Heinemann, 1973), p. 24.

6 The 'imaginary situation' is imaginary in the sense that a reader must imagine it. It may by fictive or non-fictive. The 'practical situation' is so in the sense that it is the actual environment in which reading takes place, and physically connected with wider aspects of the reader's practical everyday life.

7 'Reglossing' is explained further in the Glossary.

8 See Deirdre Burton, 'Analysing Spoken Discourse' in Malcolm Coulthard and Martin Montgomery (eds) *Studies in Discourse Analysis* (London: Routledge and Kegan Paul, 1981), pp. 61–81.

9 See Glossary. 'Discourse' is used to refer to a linguistic level, and is thus not quite the same as 'discourse' in writers such as Foucault and Kristeva, who use the term to mean text-type.

10 The treatment of this aspect of textuality is at odds with Derridan approaches, except that the relation between script and performance does correspond to their much more far-reaching interpretation of the relation between writing and speech. In a systemic approach there is a crucial difference, neglected by Derrida, between linguistic form and linguistic interpretation of form (i.e. the level of discourse); and between speech and writing, both at the same level of 'substance' (or physical manifestation of language). Both the typical and untypical interpretations of a stretch of language are aspects of discourse. It is a confusion to relate the typical meaning of a word or structure more closely to form (grammar and voca-bulary) or substance than to the untypical meaning.

11 James D. McCarthy, *Death and Anxiety: the loss of the self* (New York: Gardner Press, 1980), p. 115.

12 Mbulelo Vizikhungo Mzamane, *Black Consciousness Poets in South Africa, 1967–1980, with Special Reference to Mongane Serote and Sipho Sepamla* (Unpublished Ph.D. thesis, University of Sheffield, 1982), p. 90.

13 Noel C. Manganyi, *Alienation and the Body in Racist Society: a Study of the Society that Invented Soweto* (New York: NOK Publishers, 1977), pp. 32–33.

14 *Black Consciousness Poets in South Africa*, pp. 90ff.

15 This essay was written with the text in Robert Royston's *Black Poets in South Africa* as its basis. In Mbulelo Mzamane's Mongane Wally Serote, *Selected Poems* (Johannesburg: Ad Donker, 1982), p. 19, the word 'baas' in line 19 is, in fact, capitalised. The causal spelling of 'awright', is the same as in Royston's edition, however.

16 Samih al-Quasim, 'Travel Tickets' in Jon Silkin, Lorna Tracy, David

MacDuff (eds), *Stand*, Volume 22, No. 1 (Newcastle), p. 8. Also in Abdullah al-Udhari (tr.) *Victims of a Map: Samih Al-Qasim, Adonis, Mahmud Darwish* (London: Al Saqi Books, 1984), p. 59.

17 Gwyn Williams (ed.), *Welsh Poems: Sixth Century to 1600* (London: Faber, 1973), p. 11.

18 Mbulelo Mzamane, 'The Uses of Traditional Oral Forms in Black South African Literature' in Landeg White and Tim Couzens, *Literature and Society in South Africa* (Harlow: Longman), pp. 152–5.

19 See Solomon Ivasere, 'African Oral Tradition – Criticism as Performance: A Ritual', in Eldred Jones (ed.) *African Literature Today, No. 11* (London: Heinemann, 1980), pp. 169–74.

20 There is no need of this in the performance of 'The Actual Dialogue'. All an actor needs to do to make the poem fulfil the interpretation put forward in this essay is simply to adopt, as a black man, a South African white English accent for the passages which are cited from white liberal kinds of texts.

21 Bertolt Brecht, in John Willet (ed.) *Brecht on Theatre: The Development of an Aesthetic* (London: Eyre Methuen, 1974), p. 121.

22 The conception of poetry on which this essay is based has something in common with French semiology and deconstruction, but the differences are more important, especially the implicit rejection of the idea that the composer of a text can be left out of account by the reader. This idea was encapsulated in Roland Barthes' slogan, 'the death of the author'. It is not a view with which many poets sympathise, though it does draw attention to the complexity of the relation between the poet and his reader, a complexity often neglected. See Roland Barthes, *Image-Music-Text*, tr. Stephen Heath (London: Fontana) p. 146.

23 The phrase comes from the philosopher Gilbert Ryle.

24 M.A.K. Halliday, *An Introduction to Functional Grammar* (London: Edward Arnold, 1985), pp. 192–248.

CHAPTER 7

Simplicity, Accessibility and Discourse in African Poetry

Introduction

In what follows a passage from Okot p'Bitek's 'Song of Lawino' will be taken as a sample of so-called 'simple' poetry derived from the African oral tradition.

We need to distinguish between linguistic simplicity and interpretive accessibility, and to set these within the demands of poetic discourse. A poet may be grammatically simple yet hard to understand; he may be grammatically complex yet comprehensible to those who know the subject matter and the culture. He may be both simple and accessible and yet fail to produce the kind of text we should call a poem.

Although p'Bitek does derive his style from oral Acoli poetry, the traits of that style, as they come out in English, are not distinctly African, except in the trivial sense that the words refer to such things as calabashes and pumpkins. Its stylistic traits can be found elsewhere.

Further, the accessibility of p'Bitek depends partly on the simplicity of aspects of his language, but also on his reliance on cultural stereotypes. From a socialist perspective this kind of accessibility is problematic, since the socialist poet or reader will want to explore, at least to some extent, new ideas and to question received norms and stereotypes.

Since many of the stylistic traits to be found in p'Bitek and his followers can also be found in other poets, who have a socialist perspective, the African socialist poet may find them a more useful model than p'Bitek for developing a poetry which combines relative simplicity and accessibility with innovative content.

The following passage is taken as an example, not of p'Bitek's style as a whole, but of 'simple' poetry.

Her lips are red hot	1
Like glowing charcoal,	2
She resembles the wild cat	3
That has dipped its mouth in blood,	4
Her mouth is like raw yaws	5
It looks like an open ulcer	6
Like the mouth of a fiend.	7
Tina dusts powder on her face	8
And it looks so pale.	9
She resembles the wizard	10
Getting ready for the midnight dance	11
She dusts the ash-dirt all over her face.	12
And when a little sweat	13
Begins to appear on her body	14
She looks like the guinea fowl![1]	15

A more formal analysis of the grammar of the passage than will be used here is provided in the appendix to this chapter. These remarks can be read against it by the reader who is interested in the details.

The term 'simple' will be taken to refer to linguistic structures, mainly grammatical, which can be analysed. Hence it can be used with some exactness. We can look at various units of grammar and ask ourselves whether they might have been simpler, or more complex, in specifiable ways. The clause that takes up lines 3 and 4 can thus be looked at as being simple as far as its subject and predicator go, but less so in its complement.[2]

(1) She	resembles	the wild cat that has dipped its mouth in blood
Subject	*Predicator*	*Complement*

The subject could hardly contain less than its one word, nor could the predicator. They are as simple as it is possible to be. But the complement certainly might have been simpler. p'Bitek might have written

(2) She resembles the cat

had he wanted maximum simplicity. This structure is simple in two further senses: in that it comprises one free (independent) clause, where it might have formed part of a complex sentence; and in that it contains only three word-groups.

Simplicity, then, relates to matters of structure. To a certain extent the concept is applicable to discourse structure too. The passage is discoursally simple in the sense that the same basic speech act is repeated some seven times, each time involving a comparison with the force of insult; and nearly all the clauses are attributive and contain a pivotal element with the sense of 'resemble'.[3]

'Accessibility' is less easy to pin down than simplicity because it is non-structural, and relative to cultural and other knowledge in the particular reader. It is enhanced by simplicity of structure, and there is an area where the two concepts are not clearly differentiable. For example, the fact that the complex complements are accessible (to an imaginary 'normal' literate reader) can be accounted for, in part, by their structural positioning, – that is, by their coming at the ends, and not requiring the reader to store information. (3) differs from (1) primarily in accessibility, but this cannot be detached from the difference in structural sequence.

(3) The wild cat that has dipped its mouth in blood resembles her

Here the reader does have to store information. On the whole accessibility is more closely related to vocabulary options than to structure, in particular to vocabulary familiarity, even though we sometimes do talk of 'simple' vocabulary. (1) might have been less accessible in the sense of less familiar without being any less simple in structure, for example, had p'Bitek written

(4) She resembles the serval

Accessibility is connected to intertextuality. The word 'serval' occurs in specialist texts in English, whereas 'wild' and 'cat' are common in any number of text types, and so more likely to have been encountered. However, in Acoli, there are, no doubt, names for different kinds of wild cat, well-known to rural people, and equally familiar yet more precise in meaning than 'wild cat', the English accessible word.

Not much harm is done by someone's lumping together simplicity and accessibility and talking about 'simple language'. The distinction is drawn here partly for the sake of accuracy, since some of p'Bitek's structures are not, objectively, simple; and partly because it will be used later to compare this passage with passages which are structurally simple like it, but less accessible because less dependent on stereotypes. p'Bitek relies, of course, on a simplified contrast between a traditional Acoli woman (who has no knowledge of such things as gas-cookers) and a half-baked imitator of foreign customs, who is her rival. These are cartoon figures which have their point and their impact, chauvinistic and sexist as they are. They are accessible because of this, because they require little thought or adjustment of opinion to laugh at, to feel comforted by. This is not to deny their pertinence to post-colonial Africa, but to bring out p'Bitek's culturalist perspective.

The Conventions of Poetic Discourse

The assumptions made in this essay about poetic discourse are summarised in Chapter 1. The most important is that a poem is a type of text in which the audience has to derive meanings from the linguistic medium itself as well as, and simultaneously to, interpreting the referential content of the text. In formally marked verse in rhyme and metre, the difference between a poem and a piece of prose is not difficult to recognise. But most African poets write in free verse in English; hence they rely either on other means of highlighting the medium, or on the reader's looking *into* the language without overt prompting. p'Bitek's language is striking in its use of simile and metaphor, and in the strong grammatical parallelism. Also, less obtrusively, he repays a close contemplation of his language. For example, we notice that Lawino's own village background forms the basis for all her comparisons in describing Clementine's foreign habits. To Clementine (and to Ocol, Lawino's husband) village life is 'primitive' and 'savage'. But to Lawino, Clementine's application of foreign make-up makes *her* look primitive and savage, like a being from the depths of the forest. Trying to be attractive, she succeeds in being repulsive, like blood, ulcers, and so on. For example, the comparison in line 12 uses 'ash-dirt' to describe Clementine's luxury face-powder. Here, at the close verbal level, the vocabulary usually used to describe indigenous rubbish is transferred so that it now indicates foreign luxury. This typically poetic tinkering with the deeper structures of the language brings out at the linguistic level the wider thematic contrast in the poem as a whole, between foreign and indigenous, between luxury and rubbish.[4]

p'Bitek thus manages to reconcile the demands of poetic discourse with simplicity of form and accessibility of meaning. As has been endlessly pointed out, there are African poets who solve the discourse problem by means of techniques which involve great complexity of language and severe inaccessibility.[5] It is less often pointed out, however, that the opposite occurs; poets produce texts which, simple and accessible as they may be, do not amount to poems.

It can be argued that the use of grammatical parallelism, and reiterated vocabulary such as we see in p'Bitek here is a common characteristic of African oral poetry (as it is not of most written European poetry). Yet it would be misleading to see anything specifically African in this technique. It is common in all oral poetries, connected to the oral mode of composition as such. In this context it is particularly useful both as an aid to composition and to aural comprehension. In all kinds of texts, repetition is a common way of ensuring that information gets through. And it may be speculated, if not strictly argued, that the techniques we associate with poetry in fact evolved *so as* to ensure aural accessibility (and survival) while at the same time they directed attention to the fact of utterance, *how* we speak *as* we speak. Poetry, among other things, reminds us of the fact that we speak a language, that is, that we are human.

A Functional Perspective on Technique

If it can be accepted that the poet's technique relates to his discoursal aims and conventions, it follows that the modern African poet's search for models ought to be shaped by these, particularly by his aims, rather than by the oral tradition just because that also happens to contain simple and/or accessible poetry. The socialist poet, in particular, does not have exactly the same aims as the oral poet of his past; and although he will profit from studying p'Bitek, he will learn as much at least from poets who approach compositional problems from a socialist perspective, and who also aim at a simple and accessible style. Idi Bukar's[6] work is instructive since he has benefited from a study of Eastern European poets such as Miroslav Holub,[7] and perhaps the Cuban poet, Nicolas Guillen.[8] It is instructive because the main difference between the culturalist and Marxist approaches to African literature lies in their contrasting attitudes to so-called 'foreign ideologies'. The movement in university literary studies since the early seventies has been of a mainly culturalist type, emphasising African writers, as opposed to English or American, no matter what their ideologies are. A socialist perspective, however, will surely study work from all parts of the world, especially poetry written in a socialist context, adapting to their own concrete circumstances. Consider, for example, the simplicity and accessibility of the following lines by Brecht.

But at that time will be praised
Those who sat on the bare ground to write
Those who sat among the lowly

Those who sat with the fighters.
Those who reported the sufferings of the lowly
Those who reported the deeds of the fighters
With art. In the noble words
Formerly reserved
For the adulation of Kings.[9]

The need to place the subjects of the clause in a list after the predicator, 'will be praised' leads to some unfamiliar form in the first line, but apart from that the language is both simple and easily accessible. The poem is stylistically very similar to a (translated) African praise song except that Brecht has turned upside-down the conventional idea that those to be praised are the big men, for whom the fine words are indeed traditionally 'reserved'. Such an idea is novel, will no doubt offend a number of old men in a village audience, and hence requires some readjustment by the audience of received stereotypes.

Here is another example of the use of parallelism by Holub, who, a professor of pathology, can write that 'most of all I like writing for people untouched by poetry'.[10] In the following passage he is speaking of the misuse of power by a tyrant, which he describes, *strangely*, in terms of cleanliness.

Clean as the map of an unnecessary battle,
Clean as the anatomy of a hyena,
Clean as the conscience of a gun,
Clean as the hands that run a slaughter-house,
Clean as the king of ants,
Pure as the sperm of Genghis Khan,
Clean as the spore of anthrax,
Clean as the bare behind of death.[11]

This is grammatically simple but not so accessible as the Brecht or p'Bitek passages. The obscurity in an African context of 'Genghis Khan' would not be paralleled in Czechoslovakia – a reminder that inaccessibility is culturally relative. A more significant kind of inaccessibility in the passage is that apparent incongruity of calling these vile things 'clean'. Holub here is redefining a word to bring out an irony. 'Clean' can be used to mean 'innocent', and by extension, uninvolved, indifferent, detached. The 'clean' hands of the tyrant, like those of the man who runs the slaughter-house (and probably does not actually kill animals) are deceptive. This is because men have to bear responsibility for what they do at a distance; the effect of an evil action or decision is not like that of a natural process, which simply happens.

This passage, and the meanings behind the use of 'clean', cannot be grasped with the same ease that we grasp a commonly-held assumption or a cultural stereotype. The poet aims to *question* such assumptions and stereotypes. Hence his teaching is different from that of the traditional teacher, since he gives the audience something more like a puzzle, a partly-answered question, a difficulty, not a set of solutions or injunctions. He invites his audience to turn over his words, to suck the full significance from them, analogously perhaps to the poser of a riddle. While most of the passage is both simple and accessible, there are points – the occurrences of the word 'clean' – where accessibility is deliberately and pointedly denied. And this is because the poet aims to draw his audience into a kind of conversation, to allow them their role in interpreting the text actively. A socialist teacher must, of course, aim not simply to impart socialist doctrines and answers, but to help his students to develop *a way of thinking about* their dilemmas. For this reason a socialist approach to poetry should not emphasise accessibility to the point of rendering an audience passive – of, as it were, replacing one set of stereotypes with another, one dominating teacher (or poet) for another.

Examples from Europe have been given, and thus a widening of our study of poetry in an anti-colonialist direction is suggested. But obviously the African poet will be drawn to other poets of the Third World. He will find simple and accessible work in the poems of Jacinto, Guillen, Nicanor Parra and in some of Neruda. Here is a passage in which Neruda uses a more subtle parallelism and yet achieves both simplicity and accessibility.

> When I am not alive
> look here, look for me here
> between the stones and the ocean,
> in the light storming
> in the foam.
> Look here, look for me here,
> for here is where I shall come, saying nothing.[12]

Mention of Neruda should remind us too that not every poem, in particular not every Marxist poem, has to be simple. His work ranges from extremes of difficulty to extremes of accessibility, showing the breadth of experience and emotion that a Marxist world-view can encompass. The beauty (let us not fear the word) of this passage is, surely, the way in which it extends the poet's political commitment into the idea of 'nature', the Chilean seascape, the way in which the sense of individual death is subsumed with both an expression of personal emotion and an appeal to impersonality. In his death the poet will be embodied in the sea- and landscapes that reared him. There is no need of further self-assertion. Yet this idea is embodied also in the words of a poem, and carries the further implied idea that there is a kind of impersonal muteness marked for the poet, whose words, like the landscape, survive him and speak for, and instead of, him as an individual. It is also in this poem, and others, that he is to be found, 'saying nothing'.

Conclusion: Culture and Intention

The conservative movement in modern African poetry has been valuable in directing attention to the techniques of oral traditional poetry, and in the hands of composers like Awoonor, p'Bitek and Mazisi Kunene (to mention only anglophone poets) has shown how these can be used in a modern context, both in African languages and in English translation. The view expressed here has been that poetic techniques should be looked at functionally, in terms of what the poet is trying to do, and the problem has been seen from a socialist viewpoint. The socialist will want to remind the culturalist that culture is not the same as tradition, that a culture also reflects the intentions of a people, what they want beyond what they happen to have, or to have had in the past. The traditional oral poet would hardly himself have had the aims of his modern admirer to 'get back to the true African tradition' since he would not have had the modern experience of feeling out of that tradition. Also, for the socialist, 'culture' implies values such as egalitarianism which are foreign to many traditional African societies, and so imply a break with them. For analogous reasons a similar break is implied in socialist art – though there is no need to go so far, nor to become so narrow, as to say that *all* socialist art has to be either simple or accessible to 'all'. But some should.

Appendix to Chapter 7
Analysis of Grammatical and Discoursal Simplicity[13]

(1) Grammatical Structure

Clause	Connecting Adjunct	Subject	Predicator	Complement	Adjunct
1		Her lips	are	red hot [like glowing charcoal]	

Clause	Connecting Adjunct	Subject	Predicator	Complement	Adjunct
2		She	resembles	the wild cat [that has dipped its mouth in blood]	
3		Her mouth	is		like raw yaws
4		It	looks		like an open ulcer like the mouth [of a fiend]
5		Tina	dusts	powder	on her face
6	And	it	looks	so pale.	
7		She	resembles	the wizard [getting ready for the midnight dance.]	
8		She	dusts	the ash dirt	all over her face.
9	And when	a little sweat	begins to appear		on her body
10		She	looks		like the guinea fowl!

The table above shows the relative word-density after the predicator. The arrangement is by clause, not verse-line.[14] The square brackets indicate an embedded structure; that is, where within a complement there is another structure such as an adjunct or a clause operating as a component of it. For example, in the first clause, the complement is made up of a word-group with its head, 'cat'. The other words support and amplify that word. The words before it are known as 'modifiers' and the ones after it form the 'qualifier', but the qualifier is itself a new clause with its own subject, predicator, complement and adjunct.

The	wild	cat	that	has dipped	its mouth	in blood.
modifier	modifier	head	qualifier			
			Subject	Predicator	Complement	Adjunct

(2) Discourse Structure

(a) *Ideational*

The passage is constructed from a number of clauses which are related to each other through 'elaboration', the same basic idea recurring in different forms. Each clause is either relational or material process. In the relational clauses Tina, or an aspect of her, is related through comparison to a ghoulish attribute connected to village life. Two of the material process clauses are based on the action of dusting, and one is based on an event, the appearance of sweat. In the actional clauses Tina is the actor, and powder is the goal, and there is a locative connecting the process to her face. The event clause can be seen as a kind of action in which the sweat is treated as a kind of goal, an affected entity to which the action of appearing happens.

Attributive clauses

CLAUSE	CARRIER (Tina or aspect of)	RELATION (resemblance)	ATTRIBUTE (ghoulish)
1	Her lips	are	red hot like glowing charcoal
2	She	resembles	the wild cat that has dipped its mouth in blood
3	Her mouth	is	like raw yaws
4	It	looks	like an open ulcer, like the mouth of a fiend
6	it	looks	so pale.
7	She	resembles	the wizard getting ready for the midnight dance
10	She	looks like	the guinea fowl

Material process clauses

CLAUSE	ACTOR (Tina)	ACTION (dusting/ appearing)	GOAL/AFFECTED (powder/sweat)	LOCATIVE (Aspect of Tina)
5	Tina	dusts	powder	on her face
8	She	dusts	the ash-dirt	all over her face
9		begins to appear	a little sweat	on her body

(b) *Textual*

The clearest way in which textuality is shown is in the cohesion. Cohesion is the 'tying' of words of different kinds independently of grammatical structure. Figure 3 is based on the clause analysis in the

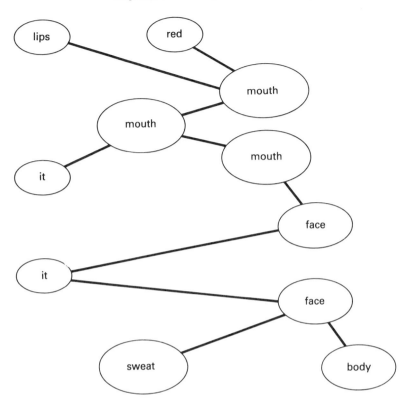

Figure 3

sense that words which are semantically related are connected, but not if they occur in the same clause. This limit is imposed to make the diagram simpler and more manageable. It is possible to discern a number of very closely related words which form chains through the text. For example there are words which tie with 'lips' and 'red'.

These are all parts of the body, or refer back to mention of parts of the body. Other chains begin with 'like', 'glowing', and a second chain can be traced from 'red', relating to red things/colour. The conjunctions in 6 and 9 connect whole clauses. Finally there are the words referring to Tina herself. The cohesion is accessible in the sense that there are a large number of repeated items, especially 'mouth', 'resembles/like' and 'she/her'. The ties connecting 'wild cat' to its chain are less obvious.

Figure 4 shows a number of cohesive chains which are independent of each other. In many texts the chains interweave.[15] The simplicity of p'Bitek's textuality in this passage is shown in the lack of interweaving.

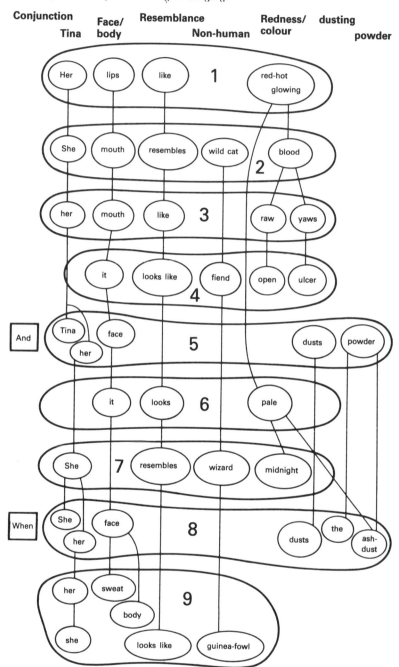

Conjunction **Face/** **Resemblance** **Redness/** **dusting**
Tina **body** **Non-human** **colour** **powder**

1 — Her, lips, like, red-hot glowing

2 — She, mouth, resembles, wild cat, blood

3 — her, mouth, like, raw, yaws

4 — it, looks like, fiend, open, ulcer

5 — And, Tina, face, her, dusts, powder

6 — it, looks, pale

7 — She, resembles, wizard, midnight

8 — When, She, her, face, dusts, the, ash-dust

9 — her, sweat, body, she, looks like, guinea-fowl

Figure 4 Cohesive items

There is one example only, where the item 'pale' brings together the themes of redness and colour, and that of powder, the word 'ash-dirt' expressing both ideas.

Within individual clauses the texture is extremely repetitive. In all but 6 and 9 Tina or a pronoun referring to her comes as the 'theme' which enunciates the topic of the clause, or in 1 and 3 as the modifying element in the theme. Part of the effect of the thematisation of Tina and/or aspects of her body, and the large number of items in these chains, is to reveal Tina's self-centredness and vanity (as this appears and is encoded by Lawino). Similarly repetitive is the placing of the comparisons last in each clause.

(c) *Interpersonal*
The passage as a whole constitutes a piece of mockery in which insulting comparisons are drawn in the form of apparently 'informative' acts, the attitude of Lawino being reinforced by the likely phonological tunes used in performance. The passage does not come at the beginning of the second of the poem, but as part of a (one-sided) topic exchange, beginning with

Ocol is no longer in love with the old type;
He is in love with a modern girl

which constitutes the opening move. The passage discussed here begins with a bound-opening move, and all the other clauses make up supporting moves which elaborate that move reiteratively. There is no need of a formal analysis of the passage clause by clause, because the moves and acts are all the same. Here the repetition is particularly striking, and does not show any change in discoursal tack, which again makes it accessible because predictable as move and act. This repetitiveness may give the force of 'nagging' jealousy on the part of Lawino.

The intonation of the passage is likely to have a number of rise-fall tones indicating typical mocker's amazement. In the schematised illustration below the capitalised syllables are stressed, and the rise and fall of the voice is indicated by the rise and fall of the type.

```
              O                          A
          H  T                       H  R
her LIPS are RED     LIKE     O     C      coal
                              L  W
                           G      ing
```

The interpersonal layer of discourse provides the poem with its rhetorical strength, imitating the imaginary voice of a complaining woman to an imaginary audience; it is interactive in its imitation of conversational interaction. Tina is being discussed but it is an imaginary audience which is being addressed.

NOTES

1 Okot p'Bitek, 'Song of Lawino' in *Song of Lawino, Song of Ocol* (London: Heinemann, 1984), p. 37.
2 For a brief definition of grammatical terms, see the Glossary.
3 See the Appendix to this chapter for an analysis of the discourse structure.
4 The 'ash-dirt' metaphor illustrates the 'gest' of transference, which characterises metaphor and metonymy. Semantically the terms 'ash-dirt' and 'powder' can be seen as examples of, or 'hyponymns' of 'indigenous rubbish' and 'foreign luxury' respectively, and each of these in turn as hyponymns of 'finely granulated material'. There are other possible members of this set, which can be neglected for the sake of making the general point about transference. If we take the capitalised items below to be labels for semantic terms in a semantic system, and 'ash-dirt' as a realiser of 'indigenous rubbish', then it can be seen as temporarily transferred to the other term in the system, 'foreign luxury'. The reader has to bear all three terms in the system in mind.

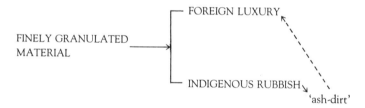

5 Chinweizu, Onwuchekwa Jemie, and Ihechnukwu Madubuike, *Towards the Decolonization of African Literature, Volume 1* (Enugu: Fourth Dimension Press, 1980), pp. 163–238.
6 Idi Bukar, *First the Desert Came and Then the Torturer* (Zaria: Rag Press, 1986).
7 Miroslav Holub, *Selected Poems* (Harmondsworth: Penguin Books, 1967).
8 Nicolas Guillen, *Man-Making Words* (Havana: Editorial Arte y Literatura, 1975).
9 Bertolt Brecht, *Poems 1913–1956* (London: Eyre Methuen, 1976) p. 344.
10 Holub, *op. cit.*, p. 15.
11 *Ibid.*, p. 33.
12 Pablo Neruda, *Selected Poems* (London: Cape), p. 114.
13 Terms drawn from systemic linguistics are explained briefly in the Glossary.
14 'Song of Lawino', p. 37.
15 Compare this analysis of cohesion with that of Okigbo's 'Distances I' on page 33.

CHAPTER 8

The Idea of a Marxist Poem: a Nigerian Perspective

I will take a particular Marxist poem as a point of reference. This is
'Guerrilla' by Idi Bukar, the Nigerian poet.

GUERRILLA[1]

You learnt to spell political words
the parts of weapons
the colours of the leaves
the angles of shadow

You engraved bayonet art on a certain cave wall
a helicopter
an x-ray American rifle
a perfect enemy in uniform

You identified yourself
You became invisible

The main argument will be that although it is possible to talk of 'the
Marxist poem' on the basis of the content of a text, for a poem to have a
Marxist *significance* contextual factors are involved. Ultimately the
Marxist poem can only achieve revolutionary significance in the context
of an organised Marxist movement. Throughout the paper it is assumed
that such a movement places prime importance upon literacy, the written
word being the basis of study, and widely disseminable, especially under
clandestine conditions.

First of all we need to clarify the distinction just made between what a
poem means and its significance in social context of situation. The
meanings of 'Guerrilla' which are relatively stable whatever the situation

of reading will be examined first. Then we will look at the most likely actual reading situation in Nigeria, the classroom; and after that discuss it in relation to conscientisation.

The poem 'addresses' an imaginary guerrilla, placing him in relation to the poet, as 'you'. It also places the guerrilla in time through the use of the past tense. But it does not place him in space, geographically. The poet also relates facts about the guerrilla, who could possibly be dead. These facts would be perfectly well-known to the guerrilla; they are not information-giving except to the reader of the poem; they have the effect of eulogy. The last two lines are not factual; they move into a philosophical placing and characterisation of the guerrilla's life, and this he may well not be (have been) aware of.

The first verse refers to the literacy classes undergone by the guerrilla in the bush or forest. The educated reader (or the reader who has had similar experience) will be reminded of the writings of Cabral or other southern revolutionary writers. Freire-fashion, the primers select politically and emotionally important vocabulary in the student's life, his weapon, the cover given by foliage and shadow, things upon which his survival depends. The second verse turns to the guerrilla's expressive nature, his drawing. Using what is to hand, the point of his bayonet, he shapes images of a helicopter, an American rifle in 'X-ray' style (showing the internal parts), and of an enemy soldier. The modern bayonet contrasts with the ancient practice of cave-art, and the use of a weapon for creating art brings together a relation between struggle and civilised human relations which underlies the guerrilla's dedication. The drawings are marked on a cave-wall where perhaps the guerrilla lodged; but the cave-wall reminds us of the way ancient men represented their own enemies in 'X-ray' and other styles in a strikingly accurate representational art which may have been a means of contemplating the animals the hunter hoped to kill or needed to evade, and mentally prepared himself for the dangers. The guerrilla's position is parallel. He hopes to capture the American rifle, and on favourable occasions 'hunt' the enemy soldier; and needs to evade the helicopter. The enemy in uniform is 'perfect' in the sense that the drawing of him is perfect (a distinction which begins to show us a difference between aesthetic and moral values). Like the ancient hunter the guerrilla invests all his own powers in studying what opposes him, his opposite. Paradoxically he identifies himself in the image of his enemy; hence his own individual personality becomes 'invisible'. A number of further interpretations of the last two lines is possible. The guerrilla identifies himself in a second sense by leaving behind these traces of his presence. He becomes invisible by his use of camouflage, already mentioned in the first verse, and by his loss of self-importance as an individual. This is a kind of identification through commitment. Finally the guerrilla may be thought of as becoming invisible through death or simply by being forgotten as an individual (except in the poem) as he passes into the stream of history.

An omission in this interpretation is the placing of the guerrilla in a specific area. This is left to the reader. He gains some help from other poems by the same poet, if he knows them. In these the situation is often quite clearly Nigeria. In *First the Desert Came and Then the Torturer*[1] there are poems about the recent military take-over, and about the Bakolori massacre. These poems, like 'Guerrilla', are in the past tense, recounting the history of 'That Country' which bears a resemblance to Nigeria in many but not all the poems. If we understand the guerrilla to be somewhere in Nigeria in this fictive history, we may take him as a kind of forecast to us. The poet takes up a position in the future and 'recounts' what has actually happened to us and what is about to. To him it is history, to us the more or less near future.

So far the meaning of the poem has been paraphrased on one dimension, that of the phenomena represented, and the argument has been edged towards a second dimension, the interpretive role of the reader where these meanings are less specific. We also need to bear in mind that poetry is in part also emotional speech, and emotional meanings are far harder to express in prose paraphrase than are facts and relations. Yet the emotional meanings in poetry are fundamental to it as a genre. But emotion also is heavily dependent on circumstances. It is one thing, for example, to perceive intellectually that the poet is expressing admiration for the guerrilla, but it is another to identify with the values being cited. Thus as we consider the emotional meanings of poetry we are still further edged towards the roles of the poet and his audience 'outside' the text; and this moves us into the centre of the problem of 'the Marxist poem'.

When we begin to talk about Marxist poetics we have to distinguish between attempts to 'apply Marxism' to poetry as such and to incorporate the great works of the past in a coherent framework, and attempts to solve the problem, what is the Marxist poet to do? His aim is not to achieve some supracultural prestige but to say something which is useful and telling in the particular circumstances he writes in. If he or she is studied by later generations, one reason for that study will be this very relevance and adhesion to actual time, place, and event. (A problem with Marxist interpretations of non-Marxist texts is the lengths to which the analyst has to go to reveal this.) In trying to speak *tellingly*, however, the Marxist poet must be concerned not just with the truth of what he is expressing, essential though this is, but also with the position of the audience most likely to hear or read his work. He will aim to compose in a way which is both immediately memorable and also gives scope for deeper reflection and study. He will hope to express and to elicit a revolutionary commitment. The term 'commitment' is not, as is sometimes assumed, a matter of someone's being passionately *for* this or that set of ideas or future circumstance. It is a term for the interaction between the writer's text and his own and the reader's actually-lived lives, their praxis in maintaining this or that social structure. Committed poetry conveys a sense that what is being said is also being lived, and this is not just a matter of the meanings of the poem on the page. It is how the poem relates to ordinary life 'outside' the poem. Thus Che Guevara's poem to Fidel Castro gains added significance because it is by Che, because it is to Fidel.[2] The same point has been made slightly differently by Berger in his discussion of Van Gogh's last painting.[3] Commitment is a matter of a congruency between life and word for the poet and also for his audience. What follows enlarges a little on this.

'Guerrilla' is written and it is in English, and so is most likely to be encountered in the context of schooling at some level. For the poet's work to reach students it is usually printed, and the publisher will take the risk of publishing it with an eye on the educational market. The text is thus passed through a middleman, the publisher, then to a second middleman, the teacher or lecturer; and both of these may be affected by a third middleman, the literary critic, who interprets and evaluates the poem, and so influences both sales and the kinds of remarks about it teachers will make. The sale of a poetry book under marketable conditions strongly favours the publishers, the poet hardly expecting to make a living out of writing poetry alone, although he may benefit materially from gaining a reputation in critical books and periodicals; but this should not hide the fact that the relation between the poet and his various mediators is exploitative. And the poet may feel that what he originally 'said' has got lost in the significance it has been allotted in the educational system. He writes to bring home something, let us say, about the logic of the present crisis in the Nigerian economy and quality of life; but he cannot publish and teach and criticise his work himself, not on any scale, at least. He must go through the publisher and the educational system. And these institutions, despite individual dissidents, are neocolonial state apparatuses. The university functions to pass people into the privileged class. So the poet's work, intended to question the role of that class, finds itself utilised as a part of its reproduction, as 'radical' academic fodder. The actual nexus of the educator/student in the classroom neutralises the content of the poem. The principle of freedom of expression of different ideas reduces all ideas to mere 'points of view'; all ideas are thus trivialised. Of course it happens that some individual teachers try to take the poem in its full significance, and try to show their students this. During the class the students may think of themselves as radical in their approach; but they can hardly sustain this belief if they focus their attention on the way the university as a whole functions. We may thus have radical *content* but reactionary *function*. This is a characteristic contradiction in the study of literature in neocolonies, where content is very often anticolonialist, but the tendency of the university and the study-aims of its students are congruent with the dominant neocolonial ideology of the state.

The dissenting teacher or department may to some extent counteract the dominant ideology by changing the basis of the type of communication involved, so that this dilemma itself is more highlighted. This may be done by abandoning the western-borrowed notion of literary criticism as a prose genre (which, as we have seen does not cope with the emotional dimension of poetic meaning) in favour of what can be called 'demonstrative criticism', in which the response to poems takes the form of replies in kind, imitations, rewritings, and so on. This is not only more imaginative; it also has an African precedent. Iyasere draws attention to it.

> If a critic found flaws in the chief performer's rendition, in either the factual content or the technique of composition, he would not only point them out, but also retell the story from his own point of view, giving it his personal stamp. His recreation of the same story would then form the basis for his criticism.[4]

And a page later he says,

> The Edos, as in several traditional African communities, regarded criticism as a creative performance.[5]

The role of the Western and the neocolonial literary critic is that of an informed observer. But surely a critic can help a poet in his work only if he too knows the problems from inside, and can demonstrate his points by producing alternative versions as improvements or to emphasise contrast, and so on. While the critic remains a kind of literary anthropologist his judgements must remain suspect, though perhaps profitable to him.

This is not the place to describe demonstrative criticism in any detail; but some comments are needed to show how it relates to Marxism. The basic idea is that the study of a verbal art such as poetry must be done practically through composition (which obviously *involves* critical reading), and through following a production process, involving the following components (not necessarily to be conceived in linear sequence.)

(a) Interpretation of social situation (subject matter)

(b) Composition (technique)

(c) Interpretive performance (recital)

(d) Editing/recording (book or tape)

A shift to demonstrative criticism – given the big 'if' that it can be implemented – is hardly revolutionary in itself, but it may begin to approach radical questions as it transfers classroom initiative more to the students, and in confronting the bourgeois objection that 'not everybody is creative'. Everybody needs to be, which is not to say that every student of poetry is going to be a full-time poet, any more than that every student of fine art is going to be a full-time painter.

The radical edge of demonstrative criticism sharpens when we look into the first stage of the production process from a materialist viewpoint. Then the student (now as both reader and poet) must focus specifically on the congruence or lack of congruence between what the poem is saying and how he/she is actually living, between verbalisation and praxis. The students' position within the unversity state apparatus cannot then be ignored.

Demonstrative criticism focuses on composition, but part of learning composition is reading and 'prose' interpretation. Here we have to be clear about the relation between this reading and the text of the poem. Poetry is a condensed form of expression, and a conversation about a poem should be directed either towards the study of its subject matter through the particular kind of linguistic 'lens' a poem provides, or else discussion of ways in which the technique of the poem might be improved the better to realise that aim. Poetry being a condensed 'portable' kind of communication, a conversation about it is primarily an exchange of ideas over the 'terrain' of the text, drawing out the implications into the explicit, following out the allusions, reinterpreting the paradoxes. Part of this drawing-out should be the explication of the actual relation of the reader to what is being depicted and said in the poem. The university students come to an actual classroom in which books are put down, chairs scraped, seating arrangements suggest authority, expensive clothes are displayed, and so on. This atmosphere affects particularly the emotional impact of the poem. For the classroom students it may be merely cathartic, and end with the end of the lecture or the recital. The aim of demonstrative criticism is to combat this response. The emotional meanings and 'depth' of a poem are enhanced in situations of personal risk or crisis when the limits of individual existence are more thoroughly sensed. This allows the poem fuller scope. The guerrilla who reads the poem as part of his study in the bush has obviously a much readier openness to this type of meaning. His reasons for reading the poem differ sharply from those of the typical middle-class student, and the guerrilla is in a much better position to criticise the content of such a poem. However, at present, the Nigerian guerrilla is a fiction, so the poem in a sense 'belongs' in the educational system.

The contradictions we have seen in the classroom study of the poem arise because the poet does not control the means of producing the poem. This is worth emphasising as there is a tendency for Marxist poets and critics to neglect this relation between the verbal and the practical. Sometimes we can see the discrepancy in the poet's technique, in the way he positions his audience and himself. Thus,

> We need no mourners in our stride
> no remorse, no tears,
> only this: Resolve
> that the locust shall never again
> visit our farmsteads.[6]

Who is this 'we'? All Africans in general? The proletariat? It is a rhetorical rather than a political 'we'.

The grammar of the poem may be simple compared to Soyinka's but the last two lines are still consciously literary; instead of dealing specifically with concrete conditions, Ofeimun retreats into Africanistic imagery with what might be taken as an allusion to Kofi Awoonor's 'Songs of Sorrow'. From the point of view of actual radical politics the poet's contentment with 'resolve' alone is suspect. Unconsciously, in its evasion of specifics, the poem assumes, relies on, classroom neutralisation. How different in tone is Jacinto's 'It's no Use', where the prospect of political involvement is taken seriously, and 'you' relates directly to the reader's situation, to the locus of commitment, the relation between books and praxis.

IT'S NO USE

> It's no use
> Your hiding deep in the dark well of your house
> Hiding your words
> Burning your books
> It's no use.
>
> They'll come to find you
> In lorries, piled high with leaflets,
> With letters no one ever wrote you
> They'll fill your passport with stamps
> From countries where you've never been.

They'll drag you away
Like some dead dog
And that night you'll find out all about torture
In the dark room
Where all the foul odours of the world are bred.

It's no use
Your hiding
From the fight, my friend.[7]

In a sense the example introduces an unfair comparison because Jacinto's poem comes out of a far more advanced state of revolutionary struggle than does Ofeimun's, or indeed Bukar's. Even so we have to remember that although the poet has done what can be done to make his audience alive to their actual situation, the determined bourgeois student can still aestheticise it into a cathartic classroom 'experience', and a text to pass the exam with.

Conversely an actual situation of struggle does not necessarily produce committed art. Okafor, looking at the South African situation from the perspective of Nigeria, fails to see this in his response to Mtshali's work, which in context is not at all revolutionary. Okafor says,

Oswald Mtshali's revolutionary poems...could be attributed some responsibility for the events in Soweto, as evinced in Steve Biko's black consciousness movement.[8]

This leaves out of consideration Mtshali's acceptance by the South African censors and educational system, and his assimilation to it as a headmaster.

It may appear that one way out of the contradictions produced by the university and educational state apparatuses would be to look for a different audience outside these institutions and write a radical popular poetry in the vernaculars. The Marxist poet himself is still overwhelmingly likely to come from the university, however, and especially if he retains his position in the university, his attempts at consciousness-raising are all too apt to be sporadic and local.[9] The university and printing complex provides a social structure through which his texts can be disseminated. The key problem with such work is that the verbal artist does not have the means to follow up his words with actual deeds to solve the injustices and deprivations he has made his audience the more aware of. Valuable as it is to understand the present crisis, it is equally important *as an aspect of the analysis itself* to have some prospect of rectifying action. And this support and follow-up can only be achieved if the individual committed writer acts as part of a wider revolutionary

Marxist movement. Such an organisation can coordinate work in different parts of the country. To do this it will have to rely on the written word (which is silent and may be clandestine), and put out a journal, a part of which will be devoted to literacy, poetry, and other aspects of politically-based education outside the educational system and outside the news media of the state. With a Marxist opposition movement the contrast between the more populist type of consciousness-raising and the more literacy-based one is likely to disappear by the very fact of increased literacy which is fundamental to any Marxist programme, and which will in all probability in Nigeria be in a dialect of English or in Pidgin. Poetry is both aural and written and will form part of the process of Marxist-orientated and orientating education, working to raise literacy, and to promote awareness of the answers to social problems, intellectual analysis, and shared premises. A movement can provide a context for the communication of literature without the contradictions involved in production through the capitalist publishers and educators. 'Guerrilla' in this context would be much more readily comprehensible to a non-academic audience since education programmes would obviously inform people about Cabral and Che, the foco theory, and so on; indeed it might be used in the process of developing this awareness. However, if the poem were recited or sung in a Hausa version in Samaru it may well be incomprehensible simply because there are no Nigerian guerrillas, and because Samaru villagers have no reason to be interested in them.

NOTES

1   Idi Bukar, *First the Desert Came and then the Torturer* (Zaria: Rag Press, 1986), p. 22.
2   Alan Bold (ed.) *The Penguin Book of Socialist Verse* (Harmondsworth: Penguin), p. 445.
3   John Berger, *Ways of Seeing* (New York: Viking, 1973), pp. 27–8.
4   Solomon Iyasere, 'African Oral Tradition – Criticism as Performance: a Ritual', in *African Literature Today*, No. 11 (1980), p. 171.
5   *Ibid.*, 172.
6   Odia Ofeimun, *The Poet Lied* (Harlow: Longman, 1980), p. 42. My apologies are due to the poet for having, in a previous version of this essay, given the wrong impression that this poem was written at the time when he was employed as a private secretary to 'a Nigerian presidential candidate', whereas in fact the poem was written when the poet was in his teens.
7   Victor Jacinto, 'It's No Use' in *Index on Censorship*, Volume 8, No. 1 (1979), p. 31. Translation by Nick Caistor.

8 R.N.C. Okafor, 'Politics and Literature in Francophone Africa – the Ivory Coast Experience' in *Okike*, No. 23, p. 108.
9 See Oga Abah, 'The Crises of Urban Street Theatre' in *Saiwa*, No. 2 (1984), pp. 16–25, and *Saiwa*, No. 3 (1985), pp. 42–53.

CHAPTER 9

Intertextuality and Second-language Poetry: Zingani's 'African Mfiti Flight No. 1'[1]

It has been argued that English is not an appropriate medium for a genuinely African literature[2], because it will orientate African writers towards English and European norms and make it impossible for them to establish a literature grounded in African cultures. Some forms of this argument assume that the English language carries with it an English or western view of life, which African users will unconsciously take over, or at least be restricted by. Yet there is no evidence that a language by itself has such power. African cultures have made use of English, have adapted the structures of the language to express their own social meanings. The idea that all English native-speakers have the same view of life is manifestly false. There is no fixed relation between the grammatical structures of a language and the ideas and attitudes they are used to represent, as can be seen from a study of the ways in which words alter their meaning through time. In a country such as Nigeria, there is ample evidence that English structures are used, and altered, to express distinctly Nigerian meanings. An ideological viewpoint such as the Marxist one can be expressed in English as easily as a liberal or imperialist one.

English has the negative merit in this context of being neutral from the point of view of ethnicity, if not from the point of view of class. For a particular ethnic group English may be a preferable national language to that of a rival African people. This point has often been made both by the speakers of so-called 'minority' languages, and by the colonialists themselves. While it is valid as to fact, it takes the post-colonial divisions of former English colonies for granted and so may seem to, and be used to, deepen these divisions. Kiswahili and Pidgin are less divisive neutral languages.

The movement against the use of English derives from a perception that a writer's and his readers' first language is more intimately bound up with their identity and history than a second language could be. Ngugi takes up this point. His argument is not altogether free from Whorfism, the belief that for its speakers the structure of a language controls their thought.[2] He claims that the choice of English by an African writer is a choice of audience. If he uses English the African writer selects what is, in some ways, a wider audience than he could have reached in his first language, but for Ngugi, as a Marxist revolutionary writer, English has the fundamental drawback that the ordinary people to whom he wishes to appeal cannot understand or read it. If a writer is to appeal to the grass roots he must write in the language that they understand. Ngugi adds to his comments on language other ideas which are in keeping with the more general emotive point of view that English is unAfrican and its use by African writers amounts to their allowing the West to steal their writing from them.

Ngugi makes a fundamental assumption that cultural authenticity – and he is a culturalist to the extent that he extols the need for this – is embodied in the particular language of particular generations. The idea that Africans might one day speak English, or some other western language, as their first language, distresses him profoundly; though such a transition has frequently occurred and is a normal way for languages to evolve; and it is the way in which, through pidginisation, new languages emerge – English itself being an example, as probably, if we could go far enough back, are most languages. It is distressing for a Kagoma man in Northern Nigeria to see that his grandchildren now speak Hausa, but it is unwise to infer from this that they cannot fully express themselves, or their culture, in Hausa; or that they have been culturally 'taken over' by Hausas, as if Hausa vocabulary and syntax are permanently adjusted to just one ideological viewpoint. There is a tendency towards linguistic idealism here. What meanings and values a language carries depend wholly on the social structures in which they are used, and are produced. This comes down to social relations: who, in order to survive, must talk to whom, and under what conditions.

Another argument against the use of English, less emphasised but equally important, is that using a second language is always a *relative* disadvantage to a writer, especially a poet. Ngugi points out how a child's links with the everyday culture and landscape around him are encoded in his or her first language, and how the writer should be sensitive to such deeper resonances in the language he uses.

> In writing one should hear all the whispering, and the shouting and crying and the loving and the hating of the many voices of the past and those voices will never speak to a writer in a foreign language.[3]

Mazisi Kunene makes clear his view that African poets cannot compose even competent poetry in English or in another colonial language.

> The weakness of this position has produced a primer-type literature that lacks profound reflections on life. In other words, the deep sense of social involvement and realism is sadly lacking. Too often these former colonials expect to create a literature of excellence in the very language of their former masters. This is belied by the bombastic, poorly organized, semi-literate works which often constitute objects of curiosity and derision in the departments of literature in the ex-colonial country...
>
> The claim by the exponents of this literature that writing in the former colonial languages widens the writer's audience ignores the factor of quality for quantity.[4]

Kunene's remarks are over-generalising and unfair to a number of African poets writing in English; nevertheless, the last point about the sacrifice of quality for quantity is to be taken seriously, especially from a poet as competent in English (into which he has himself translated his Zulu poems) as Kunene is. A similar point is made, paradoxically, by p'Bitek, commenting on 'Song of Lawino', where he talks about his translation of the original Acoli version of the poem into English:

> Translated from the Acoli by the author who has thus clipped a bit of the eagle's wings and rendered the sharp edges of the warrior's sword rusty and blunt and has also murdered rhythm and rhyme.[5]

p'Bitek highlights the demands of poetry as a genre, in particular those associated with phonology. Phonology is psychologically 'deep' because related to the earliest stages of language-learning. The mastery of intonation and speech rhythms precedes the development of grammar and vocabulary, and indeed discourse, and is closely associated with the expression of the emotions. This is the aspect of a second language which learners seldom master in the sense of sounding like native speakers. Significantly, on the whole, modern African poets have shown very little interest in the phonology of poetry – in experimentation with metre, for example.

The problems of composition in a second language are the crucial ones.

The other problems connected with the poet's audience can, as Kunene points out, be solved through translation, through which a wider audience can be reached than would be possible in the poet's first language.

An objection to this emphasis on first-language composition is that bilinguals relate differently to different types of text. The African poet who writes in English is not necessarily more at home in his first language in all linguistic contexts. If he is educated in the formal western sense, and in English, it is likely that a good deal of his academic *thinking* will have been done and be embedded in English, and in academic discourse he may be more comfortable than in Tiv or Zulu.[6] The option to use English depends on the kinds of experiences he is talking or writing about. The linguistic dilemma of the African poet has its roots in his whole upbringing. He will associate his first language with 'primary socialisation'[7], that is, with the home and with traditional ways as articulated in a first language; but English is likely to be the medium of 'secondary socialisation'[8], that is, at school and in working life. It is usually conceded that the effects of primary socialisation are more far-reaching, less capable of change and conscious control, than those of secondary socialisation.[9]

In what follows the idea of 'roots' in language will be looked at a little more closely. It is often associated with the 'connotations' or 'associations' words are felt to have. This notion of connotation can be described in terms of 'intertextuality'. It will not be possible to get to the bottom of the problem as to how poetry and poetic uses of language evoke emotions; but the question may be raised as to whether poetry needs always to be intimate and 'deep' in this psychological sense. The following poem by Willie T.Zingani is not. It succeeds as an English-language poem because it makes use of the actual linguistic experience of English which its likely readers will have had.

AFRICAN MFITI* FLIGHT NO 1[10]   (witch)

Welcome aboard	1	
Flight No. AMF1	2	
From Blantyre	3	
To Jubeki*	4	(Johannesburg)
Get ready for take-off:	5	
make sure you're all naked,	6	
don't fasten your seat-belts,	7	
chingambwe* smokers are free.	8	(cigarette)
A journey of 1,500 miles	9	
Takes you only one second	10	
Captain Chikanga* and his crew	11	(once a very famous witch-doctor in Central Africa)

Wish you all a very nice flight	12
And a wonderful stay in Jubeki.	13
Note the following:	14
Jubeki is too electrified,	15
Take care when you're jumping	16
From one graveyard to another.	17
Thank you!	18

Poetry and Intertextuality

We live in a world of texts, conversations, road signs, thousand-line epics, letters, and so on. By these we communicate, and of these, in one sense at least, our experience is made, and our sense of ourselves is made. A poem is just one kind of text which shares with others the fact that it coheres, partly by virtue of its inner cohesion, and partly because of its relation to its immediate or wider context of situation – which may in turn be expressed as a text or texts. Traditionally language has been studied in terms of words and sentences, but in actual experience it always occurs in texts, and the sentences and words make sense and have grammar in relation to these texts. Any text can be looked at in terms of what Halliday terms the 'macrofunctions'[11] of language. That is, a text will combine three discourse layers, the function of representing some state of affairs (the ideational function), of being the site of human interactions (the interpersonal function), and of having a sequence and coherence (the textual function). What distinguishes a poem from other texts is primarily the discourse roles assumed by the poet and his audience.

The reader or hearer of a poem takes the text as something to be explored *as* a text; he looks into the language and is interested in the 'deep structures', the ways in which it has been produced; he tries to see in it a philosophical theme (the ideational unity of the text), and also an emotional significance he can relate to his own affective life (the interpersonal unity of the text); and he follows the text through as a cumulative process which ends with a final 'punch-line' or clinching summing-up, which often shifts the perspective of all that he has just read (the textual unity). The reader also feels free to reinterpret the text of a poem to suit himself, to see it his own way, make it his own. The poem, he understands, is composed with this openness in mind. Just as the poet himself may come back to an old poem and say to himself, 'I never realised that in this poem what I was *really* worried about was my relationship to my father' and so himself retrospectively reinterpret, or 're-mean' the poem, so the reader can take the poem in ways which the poet may not have realised were possible, or may even disagree with.[12]

The internal unity of a text is most easily seen along the textual layer of discourse, through the cohesion. The clearest example of this is the lexical cohesion. In 'African Mfiti Flight No 1', for example, we can see a thread of meaning in the semantically-related words,

Flight	title
aboard	line 1
Flight	line 2
take-off	line 5
seat-belts	line 7
journey	line 9
Captain, crew	line 11
flight	line 12

All these words are associated with air travel. Also, they are all typical items in texts connected with air travel. One characteristic of literary texts is that they make imaginative use of other texts. The text set out on pages 108–9 above is the text of a poem, but the poem in turn borrows heavily from the kind of text which an airline captain or chief steward would speak to the passengers before take-off. The text of the poem is, in this sense, an imitation of an airline announcement.

But it is not only an imitation. There are characteristics, mainly at the level of discourse, which relate Zingani's text to other poems. All poets make use of the works of their predecessors. The very idea of writing a *poem* involves writing in the same general kind of way as the poets that the young poet may first have come across in poetry anthologies, or in writers' group meetings, or in the classroom. Zingani's text, for example, is set out in lines, and is supposed to be read from the point of view of poetic discourse, not as a forged airline announcement. The kind of poem which the Zingani text can be related to is, perhaps, the modern free-verse type. We can call this the text model. The airline text is used as a framing device, and provides the overall structure of the poem, the tone of voice in which it may be performed, and is the basis of the jokes, since it sets up expectations which can then be flouted. A further look into the way the framing text is subverted will reveal the main theme of the poem.

The airline announcement in real life illustrates the cool reliable voice of the captain or the chief steward. It is the voice of authority and comfort, reassuring but totally powerful. It typifies the virtues of white technological society and conditioning, and in the context of southern

Africa, the analagous role of apartheid. But in this poem the captain is black, and bears the name of a famous 'witch-doctor'; his advice overturns the expected white reliability, coolness, and control. The rules are all to be flouted. The stereotyped role allocated by whites to the indisciplined blacks is to be relished. They are to adopt a Césaire-like, or Caliban-like, posture of playing out to the full the role in which the whites have cast them, as a form of rebellion and self-assertion. In line with some strands of Black Consciousness the white rigour is to be thrown off. We may recall Sepamla's more explicit exposition.

> we will have to read time from the sun
> and stop hurting our wrists
>
> we will have to drink home beer
> and give up potent spirits and things[13]

The framing text is, more or less, coextensive with the model text, the poem itself. But Zingani also draws more intermittently on other texts. For example, he makes use of the Chewa words glossed in brackets, 'mfiti', 'chingambwe', and the local abbreviation for Johannesburg. Without the editor's gloss these would certainly appear 'obscure' to readers outside Malawi and Southern Africa. Also, from the point of view of the interpersonal or affective impact of the poem the use of such words will strike different readers in different ways. It will recall a range of everyday, probably spoken, texts to the Chewa reader, but not to the Nigerian or Kenyan reader to whom the words are likely to seem exotic. For him the gloss words such as 'witch' and 'cigarette' have to be responded to, and will have different significance depending on culture and religion. A characteristic of African poems in English is that some of the text-types quoted from in this way will not be in English. This point has been made elegantly by Egudu in his study of Okigbo's use of translation[14] but it is very general. Any reference to childhood or traditional life will call to the African reader's mind texts in his first language.

In understanding any text, not just poems, we bring to bear our linguistic experience of a variety of other texts. There will be a 'scatter' of cognate texts, from which the text under a reader's attention is constructed. Before an attempt is made to summarise these in relation to 'Mfiti Flight No. 1' attention needs to be drawn to one further text-type which bears on the clinching of the poem.

The last section, from lines 14 to the end, constitutes this clinching. Johannesburg, to which the passengers and crew are travelling (a naked witch's coven) and in which they are wished 'a wonderful stay' is, in fact, an electrified system of 'graveyards' which they will have to jump in and out of. South Africa is a place of death and deathliness, which crushes whatever is human, and 'black', a deathscape to be associated not only with the electrified fences of western technological and mental inhibition, but also with the rampaging of Captain Chikanga and his coven. Obviously, for the reader to recognise the force of 'electrified' and 'graveyard' he needs to have talked about and read about the situation in South Africa; that is, to have experienced spoken and written texts about it. These will be in both English and, for a Malawian, other southern African languages.

The poem, then, involves a scatter of texts, some written, some spoken, some in English, some in Chewa, some in other languages spoken in Africa. It is possible to sketch in an approximate way the kind of scatter this poem has, from the point of view of a hypothetical Malawian reader.

Scatter of texts for 'African Mfiti Flight No. 1'

Text-type	Role in the poem	Context	Mode & language
1 Other modern poems in free verse using non-literary frames	literary model	modern school	written, English
2 Typical airline welcoming announcement	non-literary frame	modern international travel (to RSA)	spoken, English
3 Texts about witchcraft in Malawi	allusory	home	spoken, Chewa
4 Historical, featuring 'Chikanga'	allusory	school	written, English
5 Texts featuring 'chingambwe'	allusory	home, street, pub	spoken, Chewa
6 Texts/maps of southernAfrica	allusory	school	written, English

Text-type	Role in the poem	Context	Mode & language
7 Texts about conditions in RSA	allusory	school, papers, home, street, *et al.*	English & Chewa, spoken & written
8 Texts about Black Consciousness	allusory	pamphlets, meetings, home, school	written & spoken English

The interpersonal significance of the text, and its emotional impact may be related to the greater variety of spoken texts it can bring to bear than would be possible for example in a poem about the poet's village childhood.

Structurally and textually the framing text and the model text, (1 and 2) are the most influential; but thematically 8 is the most influential, since Black Consciousness texts, of different types themselves, are ideologically explicit and give the ideological point to the poem, the point not being made explicity *in* the poem. The more remote the reader is from Zingani's own position the more his grasp of it will depend on his education and reading, and on his seeing it by analogy with his own experience. If a cognate text is not known to a reader, or only vaguely known, the theme or significance of the poem will be less clear, the poem will seem 'obscure'; or the reader may 'replace' some of these cognate texts with approximations drawn from his own experience. This is often done unconsciously; but if the reader is aware he is doing it, a sense of strangeness will be given to the poem, a sense that it *is* culturally remote. The use of the word 'coven' in this essay is one such substitution.

Generally speaking, it is difficult to compose vital poetry entirely from book learning. The vitality of Zingani's poem is due, in large part, to his use of a current spoken text as a frame, a text which is actually lived by at least some members of his community – those who fly. It could not have been made more evocative by being rendered in Chewa. Intimate *aspects* of the poem do tie with the poet's first language. But the poem as a whole seems perfectly 'at home' in the mainly public language of English. The thematic cognate text-types about Black Consciousness are also widely published in English. The reader who is familiar with texts by Biko, Serote, Motlhabi and others[15] will see the point of the poem more quickly than the reader who is not. Also the reader who knows such texts is more likely to be sympathetic to, even if relatively remote from, them. He will be the more likely, then, to exercise his imagination and see a further metaphorical point in 'don't fasten your seat-belts' (line 7), and in 'free' in line 8. He will possibly also be more conscious of the irony of the announcer's wishes to everyone to have 'a nice flight' and 'a wonderful stay' in apartheid Johannesburg (lines 12–13).

The reader whose English is limited at the level of day-to-day conversation is likely to miss some of the 'connotations' in the poem, not because he will necessarily have trouble with the words in the text, but by the very fact that his conversations and reading are limited: he may not have got round to reading Black Consciousness pamphlets, or have studied the history of southern Africa. From the point of view of the ideational theme of the poem the foreign reader may here have the advantage over the Malawian. A poem, like this one, may be in straightforward English and thus be within the capacity of a large number of school-leavers, yet the texts scattered about it may themselves be much more difficult. For example, the following sentence from a Black Consciousness text needs some unravelling and previous reading.

> The initial step towards liberation is to abandon the partial frame of deference to our oppressors, and create new concepts which will release our reality.[16]

This indeed is, in part, what Zingani's poem is about.

The more a poem-depends upon allusion to written texts in English, especially texts which themselves are unfamiliar, the more its full meaning is likely to evade the non-specialist. Conversely, cognate texts drawn from spoken English which is current and widespread in the society, and/or on vernacular texts, the more accessible the poem is likely to be. At the present time, in many anglophone African countries, there are relatively few current English texts available to the majority of the people, and this is a definite limitation from the point of view of composition in English.

The connotative meanings of texts, or of parts of texts, can be seen as an effect of intertextuality. The vaguely-defined aura which certain words or phrases conjure is the sense they give us of other texts in which they occur, the emotional tenors of such texts as we have ourselves experienced them in the past. Where these texts are very distant in the past, or where there are a large number of them, and they are emotionally charged for us, we have difficulty in focusing on them in an analytical way such as has been sketched here. One text recalls another, then this second text recalls a third, and so on, beyond the span of our concentration and memory. Hence the blurriness of connotation. The more we multiply this scatter and 'subscatter' the more we define our individual subjectivity, and so the more intimate the effect seems. The extent to which we regard poetry as tied to this kind of intimacy depends on our conception of poetry. It does certainly seem to be true that deep and intimate feelings connect us, throughout our lives, to childhood and family interactions, and at the present time in most parts of Africa this takes us back to the primary socialisation in the mother tongue. On the other hand, it might be argued that not all poetry need be of this emotive, backward-looking type. The intertextual connections of a poem may be predominantly topical, as they are in Zingani's. In other words, if there is a viable way of composing poetry in a second language it is likely to be one which employs practical linguistic experience in other texts current in that society.

Revolutionary African Poetry

The impressionistic notions of connotation and association, the suggestive use of language, have been expressed in terms of intertextuality. What has been said constitutes a hypothesis about composition in a second language, looked at from the point of view of the composer. The problems of the use of English for revolutionary poetry in Africa have generally been addressed from the point of view of the poet's audience. Indeed the question as to who the African poet thinks he may be writing for has been asked about African poetry generally, since it is not only the worker and the peasant who may have difficulties with Soyinka or Okigbo.

Ngugi's argument that revolutionary poetry should be addressed to the peasant and the worker, and for this reason must be in their first languages, is strong as far as it goes. But his exposition stops short in two ways. First, his description of the Kamiriithu project, and his other comments on literary language, do not situate the work in a political, as opposed to a cultural, context.

He never asks the questions: Did the Kamiriithu project actually enhance the revolutionary movement in Kenya? What is the relation between revolutionary themes and social context? This omission does not, of course, show that the cultural work failed to further revolutionary work; but Ngugi's silence on this relation is puzzling. At the time *Decolonising the Mind* was being written, reports from Kenya were linking Ngugi's name with a radical Marxist movement known as 'Mwaykenya', which appears to have had people's councils throughout the country, and was a continuation of the Mau Mau struggle. But there is nothing about this in Ngugi's essays, nor any reference to the way in which *I Will Marry When I Want* could be integrated into literacy and education programmes such as people's councils would be running. The lack of any orientation of this kind, prompted perhaps by the need for secrecy, weakens the impact of Ngugi's argument, and directs attention towards art alone, albeit a people's art.

Much of Ngugi's writing on the language question is affected by his quest for the appropriate role for the educated intellectual in a peasants' and workers' movement, and he sees it, in Leninist terms, as the role of providing ideological guidance. This is a defensible position in that the vulnerability of the peasants and workers compared to the well-known intellectual, is likely to produce the realistic questioning which will lead them to learn from the play, and from producing it, what they think makes sense of their experience as they perceive it. But it is not clear that Ngugi sees himself in that light. He cannot quite escape the charge of talking down to his less-educated brothers. This is betrayed in his apparent surprise at the creativity of ordinary farmers, about which he is movingly candid. It is one index of his position as a convert from the middle class, and of his search for a role. He and Ngugi wa Mirii provided the ideological underpinning of *I Will Marry When I Want* while the villages developed it in terms of personal experiences and traditional songs and dances.[17] This may be good Leninism, but the script of the play, like the novel *Devil on the Cross*, can hardly avoid over-simplification, given Ngugi's head-on approach to ideology. This is what the Tanzanian critic and poet, Mabala, warns against in his introduction to an anthology of socialist poetry in English from Tanzania.

> Providing an over-simplified solution can be more dangerous than providing no solution at all. Many of these cries for simple, easy writing, with carefully spelt-out answers, imply profound contempt for the people.[18]

'Contempt' is emphatically the wrong word for Ngugi's enormously generous and courageous position. But the intellectual criticism must be taken seriously. At the end of *I Will Marry When I Want* there is a rousing trumpet song in which the workers are called to unity. The cast sing,

The trumpet of the poor has been blown.
Let's unite and organize
Organization is our club
Organization is our sword
Organization is our shield
Organization is our strength

Organization is our light
Organization is our wealth.[19]

But the nature of the organisation, the type of party, the type of leadership, the position of the intellectual, are all left unexplored. If Ngugi and his audience already have Mwakenya in mind (and if reports about it are reliable) the omission is interpretable, at least to those directly involved. But the question, essentially of democracy, is never raised by Ngugi in his discussions of language and literature. After all, Mau Mau itself was well *organized* but could be taken over by the petty-bourgeois nationalists, a historical fact which Ngugi mentions as simply a loss of direction, and still seems to see in terms of individual traitors.

Our nation took the wrong turn
When some of us forgot these vows[20]

There are different approaches to revolutionary art, and the choice of language and style for a revolutionary poetry. The poetry associated with the Mozambican revolution is one, which can be contrasted in its practice to Ngugi's in being artistically more democratic, conceived in the minds of the workers and based on their experience of revolutionary work. The revolution formed part of their 'practical situation' which did not have to be outlined in any detail in the content of the poems. It is reminiscent of the poetry composed by Mao or Che or Ho, in which the struggle is implicit in the text and evident to the poet and his audience as part of their surroundings.

Poets begin to write about more than their lost loves, and even the theme of lost love becomes less maudlin, more objective and lyrical. They speak now of the field hand and the worker not as abstract and metaphysical concepts, but as concrete men with concrete lives.[21]

Because our art is revolutionary, it both dies and is born in praxis.[22]

This is an occasional poetry about what is happening from day to day, and a poetry of solidarity with the revolutionary party. And it does not restrain composers that they use a second language, Portuguese, the language of the coloniser. This is the most convenient common language. And a common language is a great advantage for a Marxist party, which needs to deemphasise ethnicity. While such a party will make use of strategies such as Ngugi's, it must also develop literacy, and literacy of a creative type, among its followers, and for this reason a common language is extremely useful, especially a widely-spoken language such as English or Russian, which has the advantage over most African languages of having millions of books printed in it. As a revolutionary movement gains ground, it cannot continue to rely on songs and drama in indigenous languages, nor with simplifications of the real problems people are risking their lives for.

Whether English will be chosen at some time in the future, in a context like this, cannot be foretold. It seems quite likely in a country like Nigeria. Or if not English then English-related Pidgin. At any rate a common language is likely to be a second language for a substantial percentage of the people, and the poetry written in it, or translated into it, will pose the problems that have been raised. The advantage of thinking of revolutionary poetry in terms of a current party, is that the texts used in and around that party will provide the cognate texts, the scatter of texts alluded to, for the poems. In much of the Mozambican revolutionary poetry, allusion is to the immediate struggle (and the framing texts often those of simple confessional conversation). For example,

I am happy
because I am a militant
I am full of joy
Because now I know what I saw and scarcely understood.[23]

'Militant' gains its connotative resonance from specifically political and educational texts, as does the last line, too. 'What' is not defined, but is understood in terms of the common revolutionary praxis, a shared cluster of texts which the poet need not specify since his audience will know them as part of the movement. Another example, this time from a more intellectual poet.

It isn't that things are easy
nor is it being easy
that's essential.
The sunflower circles with the light
and that isn't easy but is beautiful[24]

Here the 'easy solution' line is specifically repudiated.

A revolutionary programme of education, conscientisation and literacy, cannot do without the arts. It must foster the imagination and critical faculties if it is to avoid what Freire has termed the 'banking' concept of knowledge, the concept which informs many African universities and turns them into houses of ritual. Institutionalised education in Third World countries is a very obvious neocolonialist 'state apparatus'. It deprives the majority of a sense of dignity and pride in their minds, skills and experience, and it enhances a minority who gain powerful posts. Such ritualised schooling, often presided over by inadequately-educated teachers, is particularly inhibiting to the arts, and to the questioning of today's 'common sense', status, respectability and so on. Pupils

> are not asked to learn things which they can use to increase their knowledge as they become aware of their own limitations, but to passively receive a 'prefabricated knowledge' that has been established once and for all.[25]

Poetry itself gets ground in this mill too. And even the children who succeed in this system are, in a sense, oppressed and deprived of their own imagination and humanity. It was against such a system, in one of its sources, France, that revolutionary students made the poetic slogan, 'Imagination seizes power'.

Conclusion

Ngugi's writings on second-language poetry are unsatisfactory in that they fail to articulate the connection between revolutionary poetry and the revolutionary praxis of a Marxist party, yet its viability has been demonstrated in African revolutions by Marxist parties with literacy and education policies, and using a former colonial language. The strongest aspect of Ngugi's argument is the one that he has emphasised least, the problems for the composer in a second language, where he aims to draw on the connotations of childhood. Zingani's poem has been discussed in order to investigate how connotation might work, and it has been suggested that it can be seen as the effect of a scatter of texts, which in modern Africa are likely to be in two or more languages. The poem by Zingani owes its success to the currency of its English cognate texts, especially the framing text. This particular poem is not a grass-roots revolutionary poem. It assumes an audience of airline travellers. But it is a useful model for more radical poems in a second language, since the same techniques would apply in other circumstances. Comparable framing models could be drawn from revolutionary experience, or that of people's councils, which in turn would be connected to literacy campaigns. Here the the educational potential of poetry would be freed from the neutralising ideological state apparatuses which school the populations of many African countries now.

NOTES

1 Obi Wali, 'The Dead End of African Literature' in *Transition*, No. 10 (1963), pp. 13–15; Ngugi wa Thiong'o, *Writers in Politics* (London: Heinemann, 1981), pp. 53–65; *Decolonising the Mind* (London: James Currey, 1986); Mazisi

Kunene, *The Ancestors and the Sacred Mountain* (London: Heinemann, 1982), pp. xviii–xix.

2 See his remarks on the alleged racisms of the vocabulary of English in his speech at the Commonwealth Institute in November, 1984, on 'New Writing in Africa'.

3 *Writers in Politics*, p. 60.

4 *The Ancestors and the Sacred Mountain*, p. xviii–xix.

5 Quoted by George Heron, *The Poetry of Okot p'Bitek* (London: Heinemann, 1976), p. 30.

6 I am grateful for this point to Julius Ashiko of the Department of French, Ahmadu Bello University.

7 Peter Berger and Thomas Luckmann, *The Social Construction of Reality* (Harmondsworth: Penguin), pp. 149–57.

8 *Ibid.*, pp. 157–66.

9 'The child does not internalize the world of his significant others as one of many possible worlds. He internalizes it as *the* world, the only existent and only conceivable world, the world *tout court*. It is for this reason that the world internalized in primary socialization is so much more firmly entrenched in consciousness than worlds internalized in secondary socializations. However much the original sense of inevitability may be weakened in subsequent disenchantments, the recollection of a never-to-be-repeated certainty – the certainty of the first dawn of reality – still adheres to the first world of childhood. Primary socialization thus accomplishes what (in hindsight, of course) may be seen as the most important confidence trick that society plays on the individual – to make appear as necessity what is in fact a bundle of contingencies, and thus to make meaningful the accident of his birth.' *The Social Construction of Reality*, pp. 154–5.

10 Willie T. Zingani, in *Summer Fires: New Poetry of Africa* (London: Heinemann, 1983), p. 116.

11 See Glossary.

12 See my discussion of 'The Actual Dialogue' in Chapter 6.

13 Sipho Sepamla, 'In Search of Roots', in *The Soweto I Love* (London: Rex Collings, 1977), p. 52.

14 Romanus Egudu, 'Anglophone African Poetry and Vernacular Rhetoric: the Example of Okigbo' in *Lagos Review of English Studies*, Volume 1, No. 1, (1979), pp. 104–13.

15 Mokgethi Motlhabi (ed.), *Essays on Black Theology* (Johannesburg: The Black Theology Project of the University Christian Movement, 1972); also Mbulelo Mzamane, *Black Consciousness Poets in South Africa, 1967–1980 with Special Reference to Mongane Serote and Sipho Sepamla* (Unpublished Ph. D. Thesis, University of Sheffield, 1982).

16 *Essays on Black Theology*, p. 53.

17 'Because the play was written in a language they could understand the people could participate in all the subsequent discussions on the script. They discussed its content, its language and even the form.' *Decolonising the Mind* p. 45. The initiative rests with the scriptwriters, however.

18· Richard S. Mabala (co-ordinator), *Summons* (Dar-es-Salaam: Tanzania Publishing House, 1980), p. x.

19 Ngugi wa Thiong'O and Ngugi wa Mirii, *I Will Marry When I Want* (London: Heinemann, 1980) p. 116.

20 *Ibid.*, p. 113.

21 Paolo Freire 'Are Adult Literacy Programmes Neutral?' in Léon Bataille (ed.), *A Turning Point for Literacy* (London: Pergamon, 1975), p. 199.

22 Paolo Freire, *Cultural Action for Freedom* (Harmondsworth: Penguin, 1970), p. 66.

23 Quoted by Mbulelo Mzamane, 'Popular Culture and Revolution: the example of Frelimo poetry in Mozambique, 1962–79' (a paper presented to the Conference on Popular Culture and the Media in Africa, at Ahmadu Bello University, Zaria, 1984), p. 5.

24 *Ibid.*, p. 11.

25 *A Turning Point for Literacy*, p. 16. Chris Searle makes a similar point in 'Mobilization of Words: Poetry and Resistance in Mozambique' in Georg M. Gugelberger (ed.), *Marxism and African Literature* (London: James Currey, 1985).

CHAPTER 10

Sepamla's 'In Search of Roots':[1] Performance as Interpretation

IN SEARCH OF ROOTS

We will have to use animal fat	1
and not bother with cosmetics and so on	2
we will have to spill blood	3
just so that we keep contact with our ancestors	4
we will have to read time from the sun	5
and stop hurting our wrists	6
we will have to drink home beer	7
and give up potent spirits and things	8
we will have to seek out	9
black, green and golden flowers	10
we will have to speak up	11
because for too long others have spoken for us	12
we will have to laugh hard	13
even if it is at our own illusions	14
we will need to do all these things	15
just to show the world Africa was never discovered	16

The term 'interpretation' can be used of the way in which a musician or an actor realises a script or a score. Applied to poetry, interpretation in this sense is primarily a matter of intonation, but may also involve facial expressions, gestures, and mimed actions. When someone who is not the composer of the poem performs it he places himself as a secondary type of composer, either as a proxy author, or as a character presented by the author as the speaker of the text, as when a woman performs 'Song of Lawino'. Performance from a script is unnatural in the sense that, when people make spontaneous utterances, or when they compose poems in writing, the different kinds of meaning to be conveyed come to mind simultaneously; the poet has in mind not only what he wants to mention, but his feelings about it, and the aspects of it he wants to present with greater emphasis. A performer, however, must *supply* to the script the emotional expression and emphases, which now appear partially detached from the silent print, as they were not for the composer himself. The performer may make the poem different, in these ways, from what its composer envisaged. Obviously he cannot alter the meanings of words, however.[2] When he says,

> We will have to use animal fat
> and not bother with cosmetics and so on[3]

the items picked out by the poet for mention, such as 'animal fat' and 'cosmetics' are fixed parts of the poem. They need interpretation in the sense that the foreigner needs to realise that animal fat is a traditional kind of skin lotion, but this is a matter rather of the wider cultural situation than 'thesis' or immediate reference. The intonation which a performer uses to speak these two lines bears upon the cultural point, but primarily from the interpersonal and textual viewpoints. That is, his way of acting the lines has to show that, for example, using animal fat as make-up is quite normal in traditional African societies.[4] He would thus avoid an intonation which made the idea of using animal fat sound bizarre. Consider the following interpretations:

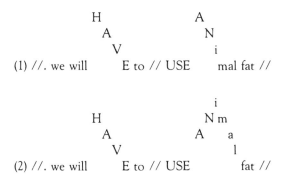

In this notation[5] the double slash marks the boundary of a 'tone group'. This can contain any number of syllables, but there must be one place where the 'tone' or movement of pitch is important from the point of view of interpretation. It may fall, or rise, remain level, or it may fall then rise, rise then fall. The 'tonic' syllable, as this important syllable is called, is indicated by the use of capital letters together with an impressionistic indication of the rise or fall by the stepping-up or down of the printed letters above or below the main line of print, or leaving it on that line. Three 'pitch levels' are used, 'high' (above the line), 'mid' (on the line) and 'low' (below the line). In (1) and (2) the first tone groups are the same ((2) might be made more emphatic by using a rise-fall in the first tone group, however); but in the second tone group, (1) has a falling tone, while (2) has a rise-fall. This latter is typically used to contrast what the speaker is saying with something previously mentioned, or with something already taken as understood or as agreed. The falling tone, on the other hand, usually indicates lack of a special contrast. So (1) suggests that using animal fat is normal, or was so at an earlier time, while (2) suggests that it is novel. In this context (2) may be interpreted as a somewhat amazed revulsion from the idea.

The decision, possibly unconscious, of a performer to use (1), or at least to avoid (2), is primarily a matter of the attitude he wants to convey towards the idea of using animal fat, and so is primarily interpersonal. But clearly the interpretation needs to take into account the historical fact that for centuries animal fat has been the way in which Africans moisten their skin, partly to prevent it cracking and partly for cosmetic reasons. The wider, indeed thematic idea, of the traditional culture is a matter of ideation, of *what* the poem is about. This is gestured towards by performance, but not directly interpreted; it is this ideational layer of the discourse which is 'in' the written script. The mention of immediate contextual items such as animal fat, cosmetics, and other things such as the sun, processes such as drinking and seeking, and so forth are all more or less directly expressed by the vocabulary of the poem, and can be read off from the script. The theme is not directly expressed, and has to be contemplated; but again this cannot be indicated directly in intonation, as can amazement, or anger, or kinds of emphasis. This wider philosophical/ideational kind of meaning is the one which critical essays tend to deal with, since it lends itself to prose analysis and elaboration.

A further example of the need for philosophical elaboration, from the point of view of the relative stranger to South Africa, occurs in lines 9 and 10,

> We will have to seek out
> black, green and golden flowers

In an immediate sense, of course, the meanings of the words in the second line of the quotation are self-evident, and cannot be changed by any kind of performance. But at the wider range of meaning, what may be almost as self-evident to the ANC supporter may not necessarily be to the reader from outside the country. The colours mentioned are those of the ANC flag. The injunction to look for these 'flowers' thus has a double meaning, to return to traditional rural norms of life and beauty, and also to seek the *flowering* of ANC action. Again, clearly, no kind of intonation can convey this wider meaning to the audience. What can be done intonationally, is to draw the audience's attention to these colours, so as to signal 'ponder these words, they express more than they may seem to on the surface'. The amount of emphasis, and the kind of pondering, will differ in relation to different audiences. The fact that it is possible, however meaningfully the performer articulates these words, for an audience not to realise the ANC colours are being alluded to, shows that this is primarily an ideational, or philosophical, dimension of meaning.

The placing of special emphasis on a passage, or particular words, is primarily connected to the textual function of language, the way in which one aspect of the text is connected to another, including the way the textual surface relates to its deeper levels. Line 10 can be made to sound thematically significant, requiring elaboration by the audience, by splitting it up into more units of information than would be expected otherwise. An 'information unit' is equivalent to a 'tone group'. Consider the following possible renderings, following 'we will have to seek out':

```
       B           G              G               F
         L           R              O               L
           A           E              L               O
             C           E              D               W
   (3) //       K //         N // and       en // . //        ers //


                                             F
       B    K   G    N       G    en    L
         L  C     R  E          O  D        O
   (4) //    A     //    E    // and    L     //      Wers //
```

The interpretation in (4) corresponds to the most usual way of dealing with lists in English, and so is the unmarked, or expected, kind of rendering. However, it is more emphatic in its enumeration than would be the equally possible:

(5) // BLACK GREEN and GOLDen   ers //

in which the colour words are not 'tonic'. In (5) the tonic emphasis falls
on 'flowers', and the colours are, relatively speaking, hurried over. (5) is
the performance least likely to be adopted and least able to draw
attention to the further significance to be seen in these, as opposed to
other, colours. It suggests that black flowers are normal, too. (4) gives due
weight to the individual colours, and would no doubt be adequate before
an 'inner' audience of people closely connected to the ANC, hence the
more likely committed to its aspirations.

Interpretation (3), however, is also slightly unorthodox in that the fall-
rises on the colour words are now replaced by falls. Conventionally the
fall-rise indicates, among other things, 'more to come' and so invites the
hearer to continue attending till the end of the contour (or group of tone-
groups), which will be realised usually by a fall. Here each colour word is
treated as a completeness in itself; it is a 'roll-call' intonation, calling off
the significant colours one by one. The status of the colours is thus
equated with that of 'flowers', which grammatically they depend on.
Intonationally (3) could end after any of the words. Hence, in (3) the
information is relatively more broken-up, and made more 'visible' by
relatively unorthodox tones. Then, after the last of the colour epithets
there is a blank tone-group, or a pause in which a silent beat may be
imagined, before 'flowers' is uttered.

The silence is a form of suspension, and may suggest that the performer
is hesitating about the next word he will use, that perhaps he had in mind
some other term than 'flowers', which he does eventually opt for. He
gives it a low pitch, indicating that it is less contrastive than the higher-
pitched colour words, but still, because falling, both newsworthy and
conclusive. Higher pitch usually indicates relative contrast to what has
gone before, or what is presupposed. In (5) the colour words show no
contrast, expect with 'flowers' within the tone group, and here 'flowers'
dominates them as the main point of the tone group. In (3) the high pitch
of the colour words may act to suggest that these particular colours contrast with other possible colours which might have been mentioned, and
also, in the contour, dominate 'flowers' which, being low in pitch, is
definitely non-contrastive. The performance is sophisticated here,
though. The silent tone-group in (3) exploits expectations that next will
come either another colour or the carrier of these colours, as in:

```
      B           G           G           F
      L           R           O           L
      A           E           L           O
      C           E           D           W
(6) //        K //        N // and      en //      ers //
```

Or 'flowers' may be reduced to a presupposed item and given no emphasis:

```
      B           G           G
      L           R           O
      A           E           L
      C           E           D
(7) //        K //        N // and      en flowers //
```

(3) can, perhaps, be regarded as a compromise between (6) and (7), indicating that 'flowers' is not so contrastive to expectations as the colours themselves, but still not completely presupposed as the only possible carrier, in context, of these colour attributes. The lowering of the pitch-level of 'flowers' in (3) exploits the system, following the indication of hesitation (the fact of option) by the silent tone-group. It is as if the performer was about to say something other than the moderately predictable 'flowers', checked himself, perhaps with a knowing glance at his audience as if to say, 'Well, what do you *think* follows the ANC colours?', and then decides after all, now as a partial afterthought, to opt for 'flowers', which gains a kind of negative prominence in the way understatement or 'throw-away' comments may do.

So far, attention has been directed to the ways in which intonation, as one aspect of total performance, relates to ideational or representational meaning. This relation is indirect[6] in that intonation can do no more than gesture towards the need for philosophical elaboration, and the amount and ease of this elaboration will vary from audience to audience in the same way as the need for editor's footnotes will. The intonation, which expresses interpersonality and textuality directly, nevertheless subsumes ideation. A performer who did not know about the ANC colours, or what some of the words meant, would be fairly easily detected unless he took steps deliberately to conceal his ignorance. He may realise that the colours in line 10 are somehow significant, but not why, and as a consequence come up with (3) or (4). But this does not invalidate the general point that ideational meaning is subsumed in intonation.

In a performance, wider significance may be revealed in other ways than the rise and fall of the voice. Thematic importance can be indicated by gesture, posture, and facial expressions. Props, such as an ANC flag or sticker may be pointed to, colour by colour, as line 10 is recited; a stage set could be provided, revealing together with the performer's attire, the traditional skin cream prepared from animal fat, which the actor could rub on himself as he speaks; he could move to a representation of a slaughtered beast as he spoke line 3, which is an allusion to traditional hospitality as well as (more centrally to the stranger who knows standard English) to war or murder. The ambiguity of 'spill blood' in line 3 may, however, be obscured by providing the audience with an image of only one possible referent. The contact with the ancestors may be taken as one of custom and perhaps ritual prayer and offerings, but also to the heroism of the ancestors as warriors. Perhaps a resourceful director and stage manager would be able to bring both of these wider aspects of the poem to the audience's mind. There would be less difficulty providing samples of 'home beer' and of the watch 'hurting our wrists' to be removed as line 6 is reached.

All these aspects of performance, again, relate to what the poem talks about referentially and philosophically. And intonation can certainly be supplemented by props, gestures and costume, especially before an audience relatively unfamiliar with Sepamla's own culture and presuppositions, and for whom, therefore, aspects of the text will appear obscure.

The working-out of such a performance covers the same ground as would be covered by an explicatory essay, for the stranger, on allusion and implication in Sepamla's poem. The teacher of literature or drama (African poetry in particular spans these two areas) may find an orientation towards performance more rewarding than a literary critical one. It is certainly easier to get a discussion going on the strengths and weaknesses of a classmate's rendering than it is on the rather forbidding topics of themes, allusions and philosophy. The written contemplation of the poem can, of course, follow oral experiments, and will benefit from them.

Looking at a poem, as a performed text, as is conventional in African cultures, also enables us to surmount the limitations of written literary critical treatments of poetry in which emotional and interactive kinds of meaning are neglected, because they are almost impossible to express precisely in written prose, and *can* only be demonstrated. It may appear that even here the assessment by an audience, or indeed an examiner, of a performance can only be impressionistic. This is not so. It is quite possible to test an apprentice's performance as a rendering of a particular script by looking closely at his intonation (neglecting for the moment stage props and gestures).

Given that the performer speaks a dialect of English adequately, a good deal can be deduced about his grasp of the poem from the way he divides the text into tone-groups, what he makes contrastive with what, where he gestures towards wider philosophical meanings, and so on. Assessment or judgement of performance may seem subjective, and may often be so, primarily because it is not yet usual for such assessments to be based on explicit knowledge of intonational options. An experienced judge can tell whether a performance enhances a script, whether the performer understands the text adequately, and brings it out sufficiently dramatically, and does not need to know the rules of intonation; but that does not mean that such rules do not exist and are not exploited by the performer, or assumed by the audience, or the judge of an apprentice's efforts. The existence of such rules, and the advances in understanding of them among linguists, are important for the teacher, since they hold out the possibility of an objective, or relatively objective, means of comparing different intonational performances of a text, and of a teachable range of techniques comparable to those which might be imparted to a singer or a musician, and which can be used in order to pin down a discussion about the strengths or weaknesses of a particular rendering. The terminology of intonation is not *necessary* to such a discussion, but certainly makes it easier and more precise. Discussion can proceed simply with the swapping of preferred renderings and intuitive judgements as to how far they fit or enhance the written script. Or a 'stage direction' approach can be used, in which one discussant says to another, 'You ought to sound more angry there'. The swapping of renderings and the 'be more angry' approach are both commonly used by directors of plays, and drama teachers. They can certainly be used for poems, though often, especially in short poems, the type of intonational move required is more delicate than can be managed within drama, especially prose or improvised drama.[7]

There are more straightforward ways in which intonation interprets a script. These may be subsumed under the general headings of 'information structure' and 'interest'.[8] The performer has to bring out how the poem develops and culminates in a clinching end; and he has to imbue it with the appropriate emotional involvement or detachment. Information structure is an aspect of the textual function of language, while interest, in the sense in which it is used here, relates to the interpersonal function.

A performer has to break up the text into manageable, and understandable, blocks of information, and indicate what kind of relations they have to each other from the point of view of the development of a thread of meaning through the text. This is primarily a matter of deciding which words are to carry tonic syllables, and hence where (approximately) tone-group boundaries are to be drawn. In line 1, as we saw in (1), a possible interpretation is:

```
       H              A
     A                N
       V                i
(7) // We will    E to // USE    mal fat //
```

At this point in the poem, supposing that it has not been read or heard before, there is very little reason to prefer the tonicity to:

```
                              F
              U E             A
(8) // we will have to   S  // ANimal    T //
```

The capitalised syllables are stressed in comparison to the noncapitalised ones, and the 'stepped' syllables are both stressed and tonic (have semantically significant rises or falls), and it is the tonic syllables that indicate where the nucleus of information is. (8) is not a viable interpretation because, when the poem is read as a whole, it does not fit in, and so is to be rejected on grounds of coherence. The poem as a whole draws attention to the obligation Sepamla or his performer is placing on 'we', the committed, to follow this or that course of action (very likely slightly humorous and exaggerated). Hence the auxiliary 'have to' is to be made more prominent than 'use'; and in the second tone-group it is the compound 'animal fat' rather than just 'fat' as opposed to some other part of the animal, which is being focused upon; so stress and pitch follow the rules in English for compound nouns. These aspects of information structure are fairly well fixed by the overall structure of the poem, and the performer has little scope for innovation. The poem has the structure of a list of intentions, and each item begins with a suggestion followed by an expansion explaining the suggestion more elaborately, giving a reason or some circumstantial facet of it. Within the items the informational options are, again, mainly predictable. Following (7), an interpretation of line 1, the contrastive expansion might be expressed as follows:

```
            B
          O
            T
(9) // and NOT      Her about cos // M  Tics and // S    on //
                                       E                O
```

'Cosmetics' and 'so on' receive the fall-rise as a way of indicating that they are already in the minds of performer and audience since they partially repeat the meaning of 'animal fat', which is a traditional *kind* of cosmetic. 'Bother' receives a fall, and high pitch, because it is new information, and also directly contrasts in meaning to 'have to' in the first line. If an inept performer were to say:

```
                          M          S
                          E          O
                          T          o
(10) // and NOT BOTHER about cos //    ics and //    n //
```

This would indicate that cosmetics were something different from, contrastive to, 'animal fat'; furthermore, 'so on' would most likely be interpreted as referring to the whole idea of not bothering, gesturing towards other similar kinds of not bothering.

The options the performer has, from the point of view of information structure, are quite restricted through most of the poem. What has not so far been mentioned is the wider option a performer has as to the speed at which he delivers the text, an aspect of the overall style of his rendering. It has been assumed in what has been said so far that peformances of poetry employ a slow delivery. This amounts to allocating a relatively large number of tone-groups, and thus increases the points at which tonics occur, and at which tone-options are exercised. A slow recital thus allows greater scope for the pointing-up of subtleties of meaning, attributes 'more information' to the text, and gives the audience more to think about, as well as making the text – if it is well performed – easier to assimilate than a fast reading would. A faster performance is possible, however. For example, the first two lines might be rendered as follows.

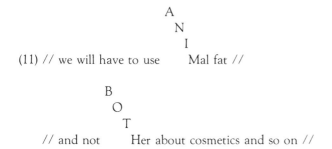

```
                A
                N
                I
(11) // we will have to use      Mal fat //


        B
        O
        T
// and not      Her about cosmetics and so on //
```

This might occur in conversation; but on the whole, in the kind of text where an audience must be considered, as in lectures, court proceedings, speeches, or performed poems, the slower delivery has the advantage of being easier to assimilate, and so of protecting the text as a message. Also, given that poetry is often semantically complex, the greater number of tone-groups the text is allocated, the better chance the performer has of conveying subtlety of meaning.

Other choices in this area can be made. The performer may prefer a fast, offhand rendering for particualr poems in which he adopts the role of a fictive character or mask. Or a performer may opt to bring his rendering closer to song and so employ a chant, or chant-like style, employing a greater number of level tones than might be used in a naturalistic style. He may, also, make use of pauses, partly for rhetorical effect as in (3), but also to mark out the verse lines, which in many poems are informational units. Extra problems occur when the poem is metrical or rhymed, but since metre and rhyme are rare in modern African poetry in English we need not discuss these. It is worth mentioning, however, that one way of describing free verse is through intonation.[9] The poetic line can be seen as an intonational unit, a contour made up of one or more tone-groups, and marked by a pause, or silent beat marked by an 'empty' tone-group or a tone-group which has no manifest tonic.

In Sepamla's poem the lines form pairs or couplets, and each couplet can be seen as an item in a list. One way of performing this would be to have a longer pause, a full tone-group, between couplets than between lines.

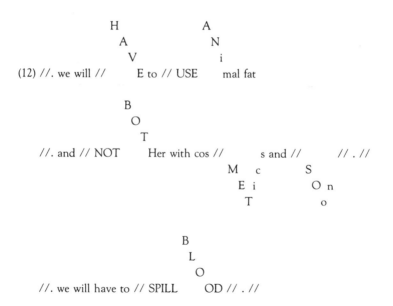

```
J                       C                   A
  U                       O                   N
    S                       N                   c
//      T so that we // KEEP      tact with our //      estors //. //. //
```

The dot in (12) is used to symbolise a silent beat. In order to show the rhythmical structure of the passage, the convention has been adopted of making every tone-group start with a stressed syllable, not necesarily the tonic, or the 'key' syllable. The poem starts with a silent beat, and in the first tone-group there is no other stressed syllable. The rhythm is the same as if the line had started with a stressed 'then', which would occupy the same rhythmical space as the dot. It must be remembered that the double slash itself does not indicate a pause, but only a boundary.

At the end of the first line in (12) there is no boundary. This is placed at the beginning of the next line, and the first tone-group there starts with a silent stress, thus effecting the pause between the two lines. Between the second line and the third (that is, between the couplets) there are two silent stresses, the second of which is shown at the beginning of line 3. Then at the end of this line there is a complete blank tone-group, which is necessary because the following line begins with a stress, the tonic 'just'. A double-length pause is then placed at the end of line 4, to show that this amount of pause would be left if the performance were to go on.

This poem, with its parallelism of grammar and meaning, gives relatively little scope for invention to the performer from the point of view of information structure and rhythm, until the last couplet is reached. This has a clinching function which the intonation must bring out. In line 15 'all these things' ties back cohesively to everything that has been mentioned, the poem as a whole, and so acts as a kind of coda. It can be given relatively stronger emphasis by varying the height of the falls, and by splitting up the nominal group into three tone groups.

```
                          A
                          L
                          L
(13) //. we will // NEED to D  //        // T       //              //
                             O              H        T
                                            E        H
                                            S        I
                                            E        N
                                                     G
                                                     S
```

The curved line after 'DO' indicates that it is a fall-rise, there being insufficient letters in the word to display it impressionistically. (13) may be felt to be over-emphatic. The performer might prefer:

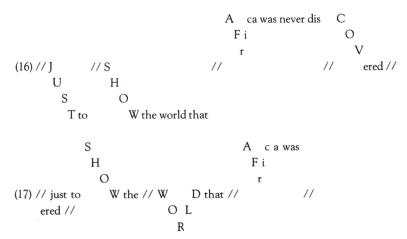

                                A
                                L   I
                                L   H N
(14) //. we will // NEED to D   //   these // T   G   //
                             O   S

in which the rise-fall conveys the sense of reminding, of 'surely you realise'.

A more brusque no-nonsense rendering would be:

                                A
                                L
                                L
(15) //. we will // NEED to D   //   these things //
                             O

Here, at the most sensitive point in a poem, the clinching, the performer's options seem to widen. The last line poses further problems of emphasis. Is the main idea to be that it is *Africa* that has never been discovered, that it was *never* discovered by Livingstone, Speak and the rest, that it has never been discovered in the 'true sense' of that word, and perhaps not by anyone, white or black, yet? There are a large number of possibilities here. The pros and cons of each would take a very long time to discuss. Consider:

                                    A   ca was never dis   C
                                    F i   O
                                    r   V
(16) // J   // S   //   //   ered //
        U   H
        S   O
        T to   W the world that

              S   A   c a was
              H   F i
              O   r
(17) // just to   W the // W   D that //   //
       ered //   O L
                                R

```
N
  E
   V
    er dis //        ered
              C  V
               O


   J               SHOW the W      D         A             N
    U                        O L           F             E
     S                       R           r             V
(18) //      T to //                  that //    ica was //      er dis //
             //
C        //
  O
   Vered
```

The reader will be left to sort out his preferences, bearing in mind that (16), (17) and (18) are but three possibilities.

One of the problems in interpreting intonations like those above is that informational options are inevitably interwoven with interactional ones, relating to interest or emotional/attitudinal interpretation. A falling tone pitched high can be interpreted textually as contrastive and newsworthy, while from the point of view of interest it may suggest commitedness, depending on the context and co-text (linguistic context). The ambiguity here may well also be related to the relative crudity of the analysis, making use of but three pitch levels, and five tones. But even with this framework, which allows a good many combinations and options, as soon as a performer does opt for a particular intonation of a line, the performance disambiguates, gives the text a more specific focus than is immediately plain from the written script, and can be contrasted with other performances.

Lastly, let us turn to the performer's expression of interest.

A difficult problem for a performer to resolve, while preparing this poem, is the kind of seriousness it expresses. Is Sepamla seriously suggesting that his committed audience should reject every symptom, however trivial, of white technological society? Does he, in the last line, mean that even in this rejection the African is still taking Europe as his point of reference, 'the world' that must be shown? An ironic interpretation, which assumes that the performer is drawing attention to the fact that it is because of Europe that the African needs to make all these gestures of rejection and cultural self-assertion, might run as follows:

```
            E                           I
          E D                         H N
(19) // . we // N      to do // ALL these T     G   //
                                            S


                                                    a
                                                    c
                                                    i
                              R                     r
                            O L            F
    //. just to // SHOW the W      D that // A       //. was // NEver

    dis              //
         C
         O
           V
             e
              r
              e
              d
```

Such an ironical 'dumbfounded' interpretation might have been indicated by an exclamation mark, had Sepamla used punctuation.

Whether such an interpretation was in Sepamla's mind when he wrote the script is hard to establish. The idea that the gestures, apparently of liberation, are being *imposed* is one way in which the poem can be interpreted. Another is that the poet is presenting a serious idea in deliberately clowning terms, eliciting solidarity. This could be indicated intonationally by an exaggeratedly earnest performance. Perhaps with a measure of vibrato, the last line could be turned as follows:

```
              O
          H   W      W    D that   AFrica was    N    r
          S      the    O L                      E  e
                         R                    //   V
                      //              //
(20) // JUST to

    dis C     ed
        O   r
          Ve
```

This is problematic because it might also be taken as a 'send-up' not just of the trivial examples, but of this strand in Black Consciousness thinking. On the other hand the poem could be taken literally, the interest being in line not just with culturalist rejection by Africans of white urban civilisation, but as a form of environmentalism. Giving up these small luxuries like watches and make-up *is* important, since so long as they are held on to, the African will be held by the false promise of European ways of living. The 'discovery' of Africa, which Europeans purported to have made, actually buried Africa itself in European gadgets and power, hiding it even from present-day Africans themselves; hence it was not *discovery* at all. The play on the loaded word, 'discovery' is suggested by the tone given to it in (17), but may be made more emphatic by using a rise-fall, the tail of which imitates the fall-rise:

```
                a was
        A   c        N
         F i         E           V  d
          r          V        O  e e
(21) //            //    er dis // C    r   //
```

A similar kind of interpretation could be shown by giving 'Africa' a citational kind of tone, suggesting the sense, 'what I really understand by "Africa"':

```
        F   a was
        A  r c
           i
(22) //              //
```

though this rendering of 'Africa' will probably preclude a similar rendering of 'discovered'.

The expression of interest is where the performer has greatest imaginative scope, and the greatest emotional 'pull' on his audience if he performs well. Poetry is traditionally an 'emotive' kind of discourse and it is in the expression of emotion that written language is, on the whole, least effective. Written traditions of poetry, of course, have taken this very limitation as an artistic constraint, and turned it to advantage. In reading a script a reader is particularly alert to indications of the poet's 'feeling'. The very restriction of writing has the effect of emphasising the gap to be bridged, the attempt, and the discourse roles that are to be played, by which writer and reader orientate themselves towards emotive utterance.[10] One skill of the writer-poet is his ability to make use of the *relatively* sparse cues to the expression of feeling, which written language allows, without simply labelling his feelings, ideationally.

The reader's recognition of the poet's feeling is, very probably, his recognition of the intonational potential of the text; and the skilled writer can often suggest this very clearly. But the performer always has further options than those hinted at by the script. This is shown by the freedom he always has to 'send up' the poem as a way of critically dismissing it. In 'In Search of Roots' he can make the script sound ironic, clowning or intensely sincere, without any constraint from the page. This is a poem where the performer's freedom, or to put the point another way, the onus of interpretation, is particularly striking. The choice of the most appropriate style of performance is much more problematic for the stranger than for the Black Consciousness poet or performer before a sympathetic audience, who will have come from an everyday life in which how to take the idea of telling time by the sun will be largely agreed. Both the degree of freedom of, and perhaps reliance on, the performer, and the sensitivity of the text to an immediate, culturally compact audience and setting, are typical of the oral tradition. All poetry is in a sense 'oral' since it is written to be read aloud if not publicly performed. The development in the West of poetry as an art which is also self-consciously a written and studied art, in which potential recital is remembered but probably no longer dominant, is connected to printing and through it to technological civilisations which are still relatively alien to Africa, as is the style of poetry in which emotion must be derived from the page. Perhaps it is in the often only partly-conscious assumption by African poets that every poem is fundamentally a script and awaits full-blooded performance, that the real heritage of the oral tradition is to be found, rather than in self-conscious imitation. Even where African poets have used modernist styles, and been found demanding, the difficulty is primarily of a philosophical type. It is not caused by idiosyncracies or the difficulties of conveying intense and subtle individual feeling.

Because African poetry is orientated to performance, and because the dividing-lines between poetry and drama, drama and story-telling, are so blurred in the African traditions, there is an important place for study of how poems may be performed, of the kinds of decisions performers make, and composers leave open to them. Most aspects of a poem can be discussed in terms of the preparation of a performance. There are implications in this for the teacher of poetry 'as literature', and also for the practising poet in his thinking about practical techniques and models. It may be felt that the use of linguistics to make this discussion more articulate must at the same time stultify; but this is surely a misconception. It can hardly be claimed that a knowledge of harmony, or the ability to read music, stultify the writer-composer of music, nor – to come back to poetry – that a knowledge of the techniques of metrical composition stultify the poet.[11] Indeed, at a time when techniques such as metrical composition are not felt to be appropriate, the modern poet may find himself or herself in danger of falling into technical sloppiness. The weakness of much African poetry in English *is* in fact technical at base. Perhaps thinking more technically about performance and poetic communication may fill this gap.

NOTES

1 Sipho Sepamla, 'In Search of Roots' in *The Soweto I Love* (London: Rex Collings, 1977), p. 52.

2 This is not quite the same thing as saying that the performer reinterprets the 'meaning' of the poem. Roughly speaking, the ideational meaning of a text is given in its printed form, while interpersonal and textual meanings are only partially given. Obviously the intonation of a text is not the same as the meanings which intonation expresses. In an influential view Derrida seems to assume that they are. See Jacques Derrida, *Of Grammatology* (Baltimore: John Hopkins University Press, 1976), p. 107 ff.

3 'In Search of Roots', lines 1 and 2.

4 I am grateful for advice on this and other points about the context of the poem, from Isaac Rammopo and Mbulelo Mzamane.

5 The notation is an adaptation of that used in David Brazil, Malcolm Coulthard, and Catherine Johns, *Discourse Intonation and Language Teaching* (Harlow: Longman, 1980), though the convention of always beginning a tone-group with a strong syllable is derived from Halliday's practice. See M.A.K. Halliday: *A Course in Spoken English: Intonation* (London: Oxford University Press, 1970). A similar notation concentrating on stress alone (not pitch or tone) was used to describe metrical poetry by David Abercrombie in 'A Phonetician's View of Verse Structure' in *Studies in Phonetics and Linguistics* (London: Oxford University Press, 1965). Halliday and Abercrombie make

use of the single slash, /, to indicate a rhythmical 'foot'; but in this essay this has not been employed because rhythm is not explored. The dot at the beginning of each example indicates a 'silent stress' (Abercombie, pp. 20,23). See Glossary for a more general description. My notation differs from that of the linguists mentioned above in that the movement of pitch is indicated impressionistically by the stepping up or down of the printed letters. This convention is drawn from Dwight Bolinger, 'Relative Height' in Bolinger (ed.), *Intonation* (Harmondsworth: Penguin, 1972), pp. 137–253.

6   It may well be argued that the ideational meanings expressed through intonation are not so much 'indirectly' as more vaguely expressed.

7   A thoroughgoing teaching method along these lines would have to consider practical snags, which this account has glossed over. For example, many students these days have a less than competent knowledge of English, and would have difficulty expressing differences in tone and rhythm, and would have to rely much more on facial expression, gestures, posture, and so on. Also, among nearly all students in my experience in Nigeria the intonation used differs phonetically from that of standard British intonation; so possibly a different type of analysis, perhaps with different tones even, might have to be used. Nigerian students, however, certainly do communicate in English among themselves, and expressively so. Once the initial unfamiliarity of approaching poetry through performance is overcome, the weaker students also may well find that they can express and grasp more through speech than through writing, especially as oral forms of study are still preferred by all students.

8   See Glossary.

9   See David Crystal, 'Intonation and Metrical Theory' in *The English Tone of Voice* (London: Edward Arnold, 1975), pp. 137–253. Crystal's thesis that in free verse a line is realised by a single tone-group does not stand up, even when applied to at least some performances of the example from T.S. Eliot that he cites (but does not transcribe). There is no firm convention about this, so we cannot regard a peformer as being obliged by rules of discourse to observe, or manufacture, an equivalence between line and tone-group. But Crystal's approach to the definition of 'line' in poetry is nevertheless a fruitful one.

10 In *Toward a Speech Act Theory of Literary Discourse*, (Bloomington: Indiana University Press, 1977), p. 201, Mary Louise Pratt quotes the following passage by Walter Ong: 'All communication takes place across barriers. . . . Provided that communication is going on, the interposition of further barriers has a tantalising effect. It teases us to more vigorous attempts, sharper alertness, greater efforts at compassion or sympathy'. Pratt's interactive concept of literature is compatible with the approach taken here, and in other essays in this book. The discussion of poetry as an adaptation of conversation, in Chapter 1, derives from Pratt's interpretation of Labov.

11 I am glad to be able to agree fully with Chinweizu on this point. As I write I have by me a copy of the Nigerian *Vanguard* newspaper for 24.8.86,

p. 7 in which he writes, 'It is not uncommon to hear practising "poets" speak of "technique" as if it were a thing antipathetic to "poetry".' In an article preliminary to *Towards the Decolonization of African Literature* (Enugu: Fourth Dimension Press, 1980), Chinweizu, Jemie and Makubuike also write, in a passage left out of the book itself, 'The failure of craft in Nigerian Literature is complemented by an absence of concern for craft among Nigerian critics' (p. 65). And some pages later they say that literary theory, or poetics, is a matter of composition as well as commentary. '...the formulation of a poetics, however tentative, must go hand in hand with the creation of works which help refine that poetics'. *Okike*, Number 7 (1975), p. 65.

Glossary of Terms Drawn from Linguistics

Act An aspect of discourse structure, and a constituent of a 'move'. Typical 'acts' are:

elicitation	'What time is it?'
reply	'Ten o'clock'
acceptance	'Thanks'

See under *Move*.

Actor A participant in an 'action' clause, within the wider interpretation of the clause as a grammatical structure which represents a state of affairs. 'Actor' usually combines with 'action process' and 'goal'.

Actor	Action process	Goal
'Kofi	bought	fish'
'Mariyamu	chopped	the sticks'

This is one aspect of 'transitivity'.

Adjunct A constituent of a clause, described from the grammatical point of view. It usually indicates place, time or manner, and is distinct from the 'subject' and 'complement' ('object') of the clause.

Segun stopped *suddenly*
Kofi is *in the bath*
Peter watched the fish *carefully*
Sometimes we watch the match

Affected A participant in the clause looked at from the point of view of its meaning. Similar to 'actor' and 'goal', but conflating aspects of each.

Nkosi was waiting
She stopped
The clock is ticking on and on

Attribute Participant in an 'attributive' type of clause in which a quality/classification is given to something else, its 'carrier'.

Nkosi was *tall*
She was *a secretary*

Carrier See the previous entry. In the examples 'Nkosi' and 'she' are the carriers of the attributes underlined.

Clinching The surprise verbal twist at the end of a poem, which places the text as a whole in a new light, so that the reader must review it all as a whole and 'regloss' aspects of it which he has already interpreted. A part of the discourse or poetry-reading 'code', and connected to the 'cohesion' and 'coherence' of the text.

Code The way in which a text is to be interpreted. In a poem, the conventions which require the reader to attend to the medium of expression, the way meaning is produced through the options in the linguistic system; and from this type of attention, the way he or she discerns a philosophical 'theme', the 'interest' of the text to himself, and its 'clinching'. These three features correspond to the ideational, interpersonal and textual functions of a text. Theme and clinching are related to the depth of (ideational) meaning and the elegance and skill of the (textual) craft, and both emphasise unity. Some theorists claim that this type of unity is more typical of western art than of traditional African art. In African art, perhaps, if this line of thought is correct, more emphasis is placed on 'interest', the interpersonal layer of the discourse, the sense an audience has of immediate relevance and point, and their freedom, in the oral poetic code, to intervene, and even take over the performance. In this kind of poetry the textual development of the poem is more like a conversation, moving from one topic to another as the audience sustains or wills it. Here textual development, as in conversation, is much more closely interwoven with interpersonal turn-taking, or its equivalent in oral performances. The poems treated in this book do not have this interest-dominated structure, however.

Coherence The unity of a text looked at from the point of view of its topic and to some extent its setting, and assessed independently of formal markers, or 'cohesion'.

Cohesion The unity of a text as a 'thread of meaning', shown by items of vocabulary independently of their grammatical relations. The different types are 'reference', 'ellipsis', 'substitution' (or 'zero ellipsis'), 'conjunction' and 'lexical cohesion'.

Examples:
Reference:
    Would you like this cup of coffee?
    Yes, I'd like *it*.
    ('It' refers the reader to 'coffee' for its content.)
Ellipsis:
    Would you like a cup of coffee?
    Yes.

('I'd like a cup of coffee' is left unsaid.)
Substitution:
Would you like a cup of coffee?
Yes, I'd like *one*.
('one' replaces 'a cup of coffee')
Conjunction:
Would you like a cup of coffee, *or* some tea?
('or' links the two clauses together logically.)
Lexical cohesion:
Would you like a cup of coffee?
No, I'd prefer *tea*.
('tea' ties with 'coffee', being a word with similar meaning. Had 'coffee' been repeated in the reply, it would still be cohesive.)

Deep structure   See under *Semantics*.

Ellipsis   See under *Cohesion*.

Embedding   Sometimes called 'rank-shift', this is where a unit of grammar functions at a rank lower than is usual, a clause forming a constituent part of a group; for example, as in:
'*The woman sitting by the fire* was recalling the old man'
The emphasised stretch is the subject, which is analysed as a group with component words, but the stretch, 'sitting by the fire' is not a word but a whole clause, acting as qualifier. Similarly:
'*Sitting by the fire* is conducive to reverie'
has a clause as its entire subject, which is more usually a group. Qualifiers nearly always contain embedding.

Subject				Predicator	Complement
Modifier	Head	Qualifier			
		Predicator	Adjunct		
The	woman	sitting	by the fire	was recalling	the old man
		(clause embedded in a group)			

Subject			Predicator	Complement
Modifier	Head	Qualifier		
		Adjunct		
The	woman	by the fire	was recalling	the old man
		(group embedded in group)		

Foot   A unit of rhythm, which is marked by a stressed syllable. In the following example the slash indicates that a stressed syllable comes next. A foot is the area between two slashes.
   // I am the / sole / witness to my // homecoming/

This line contains four feet, or beats, with differing numbers of syllables in the feet. The feet, in turn, make up a larger unit of rhythm known as the 'tone-group' or 'tone-unit', of which there are two in the example, their boundaries being shown by the double slash. Very roughly, in standard English (but not in some African dialects of English) the time-interval between each foot-boundary is the same, irrespective of the number of syllables.

Form　The level of grammatical structure and lexis in a language, as distinct from the 'lower' level of speech sounds (phonology) or written symbols (graphology), and the 'higher' level of discourse, or inter-active meaning. Form is described in three or four ranks, according to the persuasion of the systemic linguist, sometimes as having less. The ranks are:

　Sentence
　　made up of one or more
　Clause
　　made up of one or more
　Group
　　made up of one or more
　Word.

'Sentence' is applicable to written rather than spoken language. The sentence:

　'Sitting by the fire‖she recalled the old man.'

consists of two clauses, divided by the double line. Each clause contains groups. In the second they can be distinguished as follows:

　‖she | recalled | the old man.‖

The first two are made up, in turn, of one word each, while the third contains three.

Descriptions of form employ labels, of which the most well-known are 'subject', 'predicator', 'complement' and 'adjunct', which are used to describe the functions of groups within a clause.

Function　Systemic linguistics is based on the twin notions of 'system' and 'function'. Various aspects of language are studied according to the way they act in different structures. A group may function as 'subject' of a clause, for example. Most attention is given to the 'macro-functions' which pervade the language. These are:

IDEATIONAL FUNCTION　This is the function language has of represen-ting experience, inner or outer, and logical and quasi-logical relations. In the clause it is expressed by the 'transitivity' system, the semantic relations between the 'actor', 'action' and 'goal' and similar participants in a clause.

INTERPERSONAL FUNCTION　the function language has of involving the speakers as interactors, revealing roles, attitudes and feelings. This is expressed in aspects of intonation, particularly pitch movement, and in the framing of a clause as statement, question, offer, or command, and various subcategories of these.

TEXTUAL FUNCTION   the function of language of organising the text as a sequence with appropriate emphases, particularly through 'cohesion'.

Goal   Participant in the clause which is the object of an action.

'Kofi bought *fish*'
'*Fish* was bought by Kofi'
'Someone threw *the ball* into the fishpond'

Group   Word-group. A constituent of a clause which may function as the 'subject', 'predicator', 'complement', 'adjunct' or 'tag'. Groups form two main kinds:

(a) Verbal group. Has a lexical element, which gives the name of the action or other process being described, and may have grammatical elements, or 'auxiliaries' indicating tense.

Grammatical element	*Lexical element*
is	reading
would have been	forgotten
—	ran

(b) Nominal (noun) and nominal-like groups. A nominal group has a noun as its 'head' and may have supporting words before it (modifiers) or after it (qualifiers).

Modifier(s)	*Head*	*Qualifier*
the	boy	in the compound
all the lovely	secretaries	there
—	John	—

In English the qualifier is usually an embedded structure, a prepositional group acting like a word. Like nominal groups are adjectival and adverbial groups, which have adjectives and adverbs as their heads and appropriately different modifiers and qualifiers (though some grammarians prefer to use separate terms for these).

Prepositional groups usually occur in prepositional 'phrases', which are a combination of nominal group and preposition.

Prehend (prepositional group)	*Nominal group*
by	the boy in the compound
exactly behind	all the lovely secretaries there
for	John

Head (word)   The essential word in a nominal group, or nominal-like group. Words before it are 'modifiers' and those after form the 'qualifier'. See under *Group*.

Ideational   One of the 'macrofunctions' of language, that of representing entities and logical relations which are referred to or mentioned. The state of affairs revealed by the text as a whole, and the propositions and processes expressed in clause transitivity. See under *Functions*.

Identifying   A type of relational clause in which an entity is identified, as in

   'I was the sole witness'

in which 'I' is the 'identified' and 'the sole witness' the 'identifier'.

Ideology   The deepest linguistic/social level of meaning, which is realised in discourse, mainly unconsciously, in the very general presumptions the speaker makes about experience in representing it linguistically, and adopting a point of view. It appears as options in articulating 'the same' event or circumstances. In relatively simple examples these may be transparent, as in 'Strategic defense initiative' as opposed to 'Star Wars'.

   'Defense' and 'Wars' suggest different connotations – other texts – and so different general orientations in the speaker as he wishes to present himself. Ideology has to be studied at this relatively surface level of political advertising, then again as to the presumptions made in framing the strategic text. One of the conventions of poetry is that the reader is supposed to 'read' the ideology, whereas in politics and advertising it is a sleight of hand to deceive, or forestall enquiry. Ideology is sometimes taken to be 'philosophical point of view' or 'ism'. But here it is used in the sense just outlined, connected more with day-to-day life than consciously worked-out positions. The environment itself can be regarded as a system, or cluster, of meanings and signs which themselves are 'read' as, or like, a text. It is through conversations, mainly, that these meanings are imbibed, many at a very early age, and their significance is their potential for appearing in this or that text, or type of text, in the individual's experience. They also form him as a 'subject' or nucleus of meanings, and source of interpretation, the 'coherence' of the text.

   In poetry concerned with philosophical matters, a poet is usually aware of the ideological implications of his text, and shapes it in order to bring them out as the poetic 'theme'. He may not be fully aware of them, and it is always open for a reader to go deeper than the poet bargained for, or to give a different interpretation. The poet himself can be 'read' as we reinterpret the words of a neurotic friend, while by no means necessarily discounting what he says or feels.

Imaginary Whatever the reader has to form a picture of from the text alone. It need not be fictional. Commonly the topic of a poem will be 'imaginary' in this sense, contrasting with the living-room or classroom in which the reading takes place, the 'practical' setting.

Interest The personal involvement, emotionally and philosophically, which the reader feels in the poem and what it deals with. This term largely replaces the more current 'commitment', which should be seen not as the intellectual conviction that certain ideas are true and demand action, but as a *relation* between a reading of a poem and the everyday life of the reader and/or the poet. In some essays the notion of 'interest' is expressed as 'significance'. It follows from this notion that a radical reader may be interested in and find revolutionary insight in a poem composed with different intentions, or a revolutionary poem composed by a hypocrite.

Interpersonal One of the 'macrofunctions' of a language. It is the way in which a person acts in and through uttering or writing, and how he or she invests the text with feelings and attitudes. In the English clause, the interpersonal function is revealed through the 'mood' system, the options a speaker has to make a clause declarative, interrogative or imperative, and in related options such as 'modality', or degree of certainty with which a proposition is put forward.

At the level of discourse, especially in the description of conversations which are essentially interactive, it is the interpersonal function or 'layer' as it is sometimes termed, which is given prominence. The notions of 'exchange', 'move' and 'act' are interpersonal, seeing language as one kind of acting. Also, in the poetic code, the conventional understanding that the reader will look into the medium of expression, draw out a poetic theme, and show 'interest', are interpersonal, conventional role-playing.

At the level of grammar, the terms 'subject', 'complement' and so on are subdivisions of the broader division of a clause into 'mood' and 'residue' or non-mood.

Intertextuality The relations between texts and types of text. Probably the meanings of words which find their way into the dictionary are fixed by their functions in texts, and their capacity to function in a large number of different texts. A text under attention can be regarded as a collage of pieces 'from' other texts. This is exploited in metaphors, where the transfer is particularly noticeable. In 'His love-making *sent her into orbit*' there is a difference between the emphasised stretch and the rest which is directly connected to the text topic, while the emphasised stretch has been 'borrowed' from or 'quoted' from space technology.

It can be argued that the setting of a text also may be taken as another manifestation of intertextuality, since the non-linguistic features of the room or playing field are important as meanings rather than physical or social 'objects', as potential topics for other texts, and/or as semiotic components to a physical 'text'.

Intonation Usually classed as an aspect of phonology, though some systemic linguists now place it with form. Here it is counted as phonological and operating at the level of substance. It combines features of rhythm, pitch, and stress. There are a number of other aspects of it, such as tempo and tamber, which are less widely studied, shading off into 'paralinguistic features', as when a smile can be deduced from the recorded voice. The units of intonation are:

Tone-group, marked by one 'tonic' syllable which indicates the informational focus of the tone-group. See under *Textual function* and *Tonic*.

Foot, marked by a stressed syllable, a unit of speech rhythm

Syllable, a component of the foot. In the following tone-group:

// Susan has / stopped them from / coming //

the tonic is on the first syllable of 'coming'. There are three feet, with three syllables in each of the first two, and two in the last. In some notations the stress is shown by a capitalised syllable and the tonic by capitalising and underlining, as in

SUsan has STOPPED them from COMing

The 'tone' or pitch-movement is not shown, nor the height of pitch. A possible rendering is

$$C$$
$$O$$

HIGH   M

MID SUsan has STOPPED them from   ing

LOW

which makes 'coming' relatively more newsworthy than if it had been started at 'mid' pitch-level. There are other pitch-variations in the first part of the group, but these are not shown in a schematic notation.

Levels of language The different symbolic systems used in a language. The main ones are:

    DISCOURSE the level of meanings to be exchanged

    FORM the grammatical structure and the vocabulary

    SUBSTANCE the physical medium of conveying the form, speech or writing.

Each level has its own organisation almost entirely unaffected by the others. They are related by 'realisation', 'discourse' realised as 'form' which is realised in turn as 'substance'. Both form and substance express the meanings required in discourse. Discourse is most immediately related to the context of speech, or writing/reading, and is usually 'coded' in one way or another. In poetry the code (or conventions) requires attention to the linguistic medium, which may also be shown by aspects of form, such as surprising choice of vocabulary, or substance, such as metre.

Lexical cohesion See *Cohesion*.

Lexis The part of the vocabulary which labels aspects of the topic of discourse, and which does not form closed systems. Contrasted with grammatical items of vocabulary which do, such as the pronouns or auxiliary verbs. Lexical items of vocabulary can, however, be grouped into 'sets' on semantic grounds.

Linguisticity The 'languageness' of a text, which a reader attends to if he knows it is a poem, or if it is foregrounded in some way by unusual intonation or form. It is the basic feature of the discourse 'code' of poetry, its reading conventions. See under *Code*.

Locative A participant in the clause considered from the point of view of 'ideational' meaning, or 'transitivity'. It indicates time or place.

'She sat *in that corner*'.

'*Yesterday* the news broke.'

Macrofunction See under *Function*.

Metre A type of rhythm very characteristic of poetry, but not of modern African poetry in English. It is a stylisation of natural rhythm, usually related to the foot or the syllable, sometimes other features such as tone. In the following, each of the feet has the same number of syllables, and each line the same number of feet.

//. the/rain is/crashing/down on/compound/roofs//
//.and/paths are/swirling/streams of/twigs and/leaves//

The dot at the outset of each indicates a silent 'stress' or pause between the lines.

Mimesis The imitation in the form or substance of a text of some physical or other feature of the topic of discourse. Onomatopoeia is one example, as also is the use of disjointed grammar to indicate confusion, a flowing rhythm to imitate the movement of a river.

Mode Or 'mode of discourse'. The channel of communication, basically whether the discourse is spoken or written.

Modifier See under *Group*.

Move A unit in discourse, looked at from the point of view of personal interaction. It is a constituent of the 'higher' unit of 'exchange'. For details, see the analysis and explanation of it on page 77–8.

Network A system of systems. See under *System*.

Poem A text to be interpreted according to the poetic code, and devoted to the poetic use of language. Not necessarily in verse, and not necessarily employing striking or unorthodox language. See under *Code*.

Poetry A use of language to be found in many discourses, but particularly in poems. Outside poems it is marked by special intonational emphasis, or figurative or unorthodox usage.

Pitch The rise and fall of the voice in intonation. See under *Intonation*.

Praxis Everyday life, maintaining or creating the social reality in which the subject lives. Conversation forms a linguistic component of it. Lived ideological assumptions.

Predicator The verbal group in a clause, looked at from the point of view of its grammatical function.

Process The overall event, or action or thought that a clause labels, especially its central element, realised by a verbal group. In the transitivity system there are three main types:

Material process (action, event): 'Kofi bought fish'; 'The house collapsed'.

Mental process (cognition, affection): 'Mariamu pondered'; 'She liked him'.

Relational process (attributive, identifying): 'Segun is the secretary'; 'The compound is old'.

There are other processes which combine elements of the material and mental; these are verbalising and behavioural clauses:

'You are flattering me!'

'She laughed'.

The clause as a whole has a central process usually labelled by a verb, and other 'participants' and 'circumstantial elements', which can be described in relation to the verb. For example, in an actional material process clause the relations may be as follows:

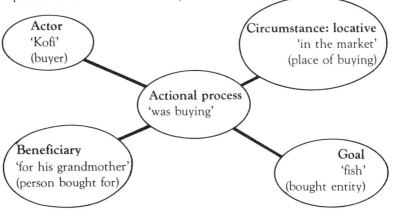

Actor
'Kofi'
(buyer)

Circumstance: locative
'in the market'
(place of buying)

Actional process
'was buying'

Beneficiary
'for his grandmother'
(person bought for)

Goal
'fish'
(bought entity)

The 'planetary' diagram may suggest that the relations are not sequential. The sequence in which they are placed in the text is part of the
'textual function', whereas transitivity is a matter of 'ideation'.

Qualifier   See under *Group*

Quotation   An aspect of intertextuality. The allusion to another text or
text-type, not necessarily direct quotation in reported speech.

Rank   A principle of organisation at the level of form. See under *Form*.

Reference   A type of cohesion. See under *Cohesion*.

Reglossing   The reinterpretation of elements in a text (poem) which have
already been read but must be reassessed by virtue of a new development later in the text. Characteristic of poetry, and its clinching.

Rhythm   See under *Foot*.

Scatter   The range of different text-types which are suggested in a
particular text, which are quoted from or alluded to. In poetry the code
requires that the reader alerts him or herself to scatter. The phenomenon is treated in Chapter 6. It is an aspect of intertextuality, which
gives the impression of resonance and connotative suggestion to a
poem.

Script   The written mode of the poem as used for a performance.

Setting   The physical environment of a text, such as a room. In a wider
focus, the setting may be looked upon as the town in which the room is
set, or the country, and so on; also, in an ideological vein, the class of
the speakers, the political tendency of their conversation.

Semantics   The study of the significant contrasts in a language. In some
versions of systemic grammar the term is used in the way later versions,
and this book, use 'discourse', that is, as a linguistic level. In the present
usage the term applies to all levels. It is equivalent to 'deep structure' in
other approaches to linguistics.

Semiotics   The general study of signs and meanings, not only those in
language. Language is one semiotic system. The term 'literary semiotics'
is sometimes applied to the study of, and theory of, literary ways of
communicating. Language derives its semantic categories from a 'social
semiotic', the meanings/signs current in the society.

Stress   Rhythmical beat. See under *Rhythm*.

Subject   (1) A constituent in clause-structure, the 'who or what?' before
the predicator.

   '*Kofi* bought fish'

   '*Fish* were bought by Kofi'

(2) The individual person as a social entity produced by language, in
particular conversation, to fit into the social roles expected of him or
her, and to carry an ideological praxis; the site or position of interpretation of a text. The 'subject' was introduced into Marxist thinking

to see how ideological orientations were produced, especially where people act and think in ways which are contrary to their actual good or interests. (2) is related to (1) in the sense that the 'I' as grammatical subject of a clause tends to give the impression that this subject (in the sense of (2)) is free to act as he or she wishes as a separable entity from the social situation. The subject (2) is an imaginary image we have of ourselves to form a meeting point for experiences in space and time; it is, at bottom, a linguistic entity which we take for 'real'.

Substance A level of language, which is physical: the speech sounds, or written orthography.

System The semantic organisation of a language, seen as systems of meaning options at all levels of the language, but related ultimately to discourse intentions. The resources from which the speaker of the language may draw. The system for the use of verbs in English may be represented as follows:

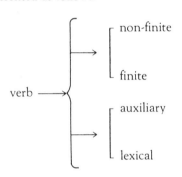

The brace means that a choice must be made from each of the systems, non-finite/finite, auxiliary/lexical. Each of these itself can be described in terms of further systems. The complex of systems, or 'system of systems' is known as a 'network'.

Unorthodox uses of language, such as are common in poetry, are often produced by tinkering with the system, for example using a non-finite verb-form as if it were a finite one, as in

'He breaking it'

giving an impression of incomplete grasp of the grammar, or dialect, perhaps to indicate character, or more subtly,

'Sun breaking over red fields'.

Tag A constituent of the clause, not always a group, which adjusts it in various ways not central to the structure. It may be vocative, as in 'Jeremy, I'm talking to you', or it may switch the mood into a question: 'This is Heathrow airport, *isn't it?*' or add an interpersonal touch as in, '*Haba, Lawyer, I beg, now*' in which each element is a tag.

Tenor The relation of the speakers in and through the text. Sometimes termed 'tenor of discourse'. At the wider focus it is a matter of ranks, roles, status, and in the more immediate focus a matter of person-to-person relations of charm, aggression, politeness, and so on. See also *Setting, Topic, Mode*.

Text The verbal aspect of a communication, seen as a whole, and at all levels of language, but not including 'context of situation'. A text may be spoken or written, long or short. A sign 'Danger' is a text, and so is a million-line epic. The unity of a text as a whole is a matter of discourse-features such as 'cohesion', and of contextual features of 'coherence'. In poetry there may be other 'para-cohesive' features such as rhythm, or number of lines in the genre.

The boundary between text and non-text or context is difficult to draw since it is itself, at least in part, a linguistic (semantic) boundary, and any enunciation of what the context is, requires a text.

Textual function The function of language in organising the text as a message through time and with emphases, shaping it intonationally into units of information. At the rank of clause the group placed first acts as the 'theme', enunciating the frame in which the clause is to be viewed.

'*Okot* was the one I was talking about'
'*I* was talking about Okot'
'*Talking* about Okot, were you?'

From the point of view of intonation, the 'tone-group' often coincides with the grammatical clause, and it is this, the tone-group, which blocks the text into units of information. The 'tonic' or main pitch-movement occurs in the syllables capitalised as well as underlined in this example:

'I THOUGHT it was <u>YOU</u>' (not Nkosi)

The clause could have been made into two information units by making 'thought' more important.

'I <u>THOUGHT</u> it was <u>YOU</u>' ('all the time')

This aspect of the textual function is obviously extremely important from the point of view of performance.

Theme (1) The first group in a clause. See under *Textual function*. (2) The philosophical idea or problem which the text of a literary work illustrates as a whole. In the context of functional linguistics a better term might be 'crux', but since 'theme' is well-entrenched in literary discourse, it has been retained here. It may be explicit, but more often in modern poetry it is not. The meaning of a proverb is often a 'theme' in this sense. See under *Topic*.

Tie The term used to label the relationships between cohesive items in a text. See under *Cohesion*.

Tone Pitch movement, which is semantically significant. In English there are five:

Falling tone:

```
        M
        I
        N
it's    E (statement of fact)
```

Rising tone:

```
            E
            N
            I
it's M      (question/exclamation)
```

Falling-rising tone:

```
        M   E
it's    IN   (as you know)
```

Rising-falling tone:

```
        IN
it's M   E (so there!)
```

Level tone: it's MINE (wearily)

The force of the tone is primarily interpersonal, but to some extent textual. It is embellished by variations in the pitch-level at which the tonic syllable starts, and its relation to the preceding stressed syllable.

Tonic The nuclear syllable in a 'tone-group', which is stressed and also has a semantically important pitch movement, corresponding to one of the tones. See *Tone, Textual function*.

Topic The subject-matter of the discourse, not necessarily connected to the setting. Not the same as 'theme' of discourse, which is a term for the philosophical idea it implies or deals with.

Verse Composition in lines, defined either by a phonological feature such as rhyme or a pause, or number of syllables or stresses; or defined graphically by the layout on the page. Verse need not be metrical, as most African is not, nor need poems necessarily be written in verse, though usually they are.

Bibliography of Works Cited

Abah, Oga, 'The Crises of Urban Street Theatre' in *Saiwa, Issue 2* (Zaria: Department of English, Ahmadu Bello University, 1984), pp. 16–25. 'Intention and Practice: The Points of Divergence in the Samaru Project' in *Saiwa: Issue 3* (Zaria: Department of English, Ahmadu Bello University, 1985), pp. 42–53.

Abercrombie, David, 'Studies in Phonetics and Linguistics (London: Oxford University Press, 1965).

Al-Qasim, 'Travel Tickets' in *Victims of a Map: Samih Al-Qasim, Adonis, Mahmud Darwish*, tr. Abdullah al-Udhari (London: Al Saqi Books, 1984), p. 59.

Althusser, Louis, 'Ideology and Ideological State Apparatuses' in *Lenin and Philosophy* (London: New Left Books, 1971), pp. 121–73.

Anozie, Sunday, *Christopher Okigbo* (London: Evans, 1972).

Asuonye, Chukwuma, 'Okigbo and the Psychological Theories of Carl Gustav Jung', a paper presented to the Fifth Ibadan African Literature Conference, University of Ibadan, Nigeria, 1980.

Awoonor, Kofi, 'Dirge' in Kofi Awoonor and G. Adali-Mortty (eds), *Messages: Poems from Ghana* (London: Heinemann, 1971) p. 73; *This Earth, My Brother* (London: Heinemann, 1972); *Guardians of the Sacred Word* (New York: Nok, 1974); interview in Karen L. Morell (ed.), *In Person: Achebe, Awoonor and Soyinka at the University of Washington* (Seattle: Institute for Comparative and Foreign Area Studies, University of Washington, 1975).

Babalola, Adeboye, 'Ijala Poetry among the Oyo-Yoruba' in Uchegbulam K. Abalogu, Garba Ashiwaju, Regina Amadi-Tshiwala (eds), *Oral Poetry in Nigeria* (Lagos: Nigeria Magazine, 1981) p. 11.

Barthes, Roland, *Image-Music-Text*, tr. Stephen Heath (London: Fontana, 1977).

Bataille, Léon (ed.) *A Turning Point for Literacy* (London: Pergamon, 1975).

Berger, John, *Ways of Seeing* (New York: Viking, 1973).

Berger, Peter and Luckmann, Thomas, *The Social Construction of Reality* (Harmondsworth: Penguin), pp. 149–157).

Berry, Margaret, *Introduction to Systemic Linguistics I: structures and systems* (London: Batsford, 1975); *Introduction to Systemic Linguistics II: levels and links* (London: Batsford, 1977).

Bold, Alan, *The Penguin Book of Socialist Verse* (Harmondsworth: Penguin, 1970).

Bolinger, Dwight, 'Relative Height' in Bolinger (ed.), *Intonation* (Harmondsworth: Penguin, 1972), pp. 137–253.

Brazil, David; Coulthard, Malcolm; Johns, Catherine, *Discourse Intonation and Language Teaching* (Harlow: Longman, 1980).

Brecht, Bertolt, *Brecht on Theatre*, ed. John Willet (London: Eyre Methuen, 1974); *Poems 1913–1956* (Eyre Methuen, 1976).

Bukar, Idi, *First the Desert Came and then the Torturer* (Zaria: Rag Press, 1986).

Burton, Deirdre, 'Analysing Spoken Discourse' in Malcolm Coulthard and Martin Montgomery (eds), *Studies in Discourse Analysis* (London: Routledge and Kegan Paul, 1981), pp. 61–81. See also Carter and Burton.

Carter, Ronald (ed.), *Language and Literature* (Allen and Unwin, 1982).

Carter, Ronald, and Burton, Deirdre (eds), *Literary Text and Language Study* (London: Edward Arnold, 1982).

Chinweizu, 'Chinweizu's Observatory' in *The Vanguard* (Nigeria), 24 August, 1986. p. 7.

Chinweizu; Jemie Onwuchekwa; Madubuike Ihechukwu, 'Towards the Decolonization of African Literature — Part II', in *Okike*, Number 7 (1975), pp. 65–81; *Towards the Decolonization of African Literature: Volume I* (Enugu: Fourth Dimension Press, 1980).

Coulthard, Malcolm, and Montgomery, Martin (eds), *Studies in Discourse Analysis* (London: Routledge and Kegan Paul, 1981).

Coward, Rosalind and Ellis, John, *Language and Materialism* (London: Routledge and Kegan Paul, 1977).

Culler, Jonathan *On Deconstruction: Theory and Criticism after Structuralism* (London: Routledge and Kegan Paul, 1983).

Crystal, David, 'Intonation and Metrical Theory' in *The English Tone of Voice* (London: Edward Arnold, 1975), pp. 137–253.

Derrida, Jacques, *Of Grammatology* (Baltimore: John Hopkins University, 1976.

Dhlomo, Oscar, 'The Strategy of Inkatha and its Critics' in *Journal of Asian and African Studies* XVIII, 1–2 (1983), p. 52.

Egudu, Romanus, 'Anglophone African Poetry and Vernacular Rhetoric: The Example of Okigbo' in *Lagos Review of English Studies*, Volume 1 No. 1 (1979), pp. 104–113.

Etherton, Michael, *The Development of African Drama* (London: Hutchinson, 1982).

Etherton, Michael, and Abah Oga, 'The Samaru Projects: Street Theatre in Northern Nigeria' in *Saiwa, Issue 1*, (1983), pp. 9–19.

Freire, Paulo, *Cultural Action for Freedom* (Harmondsworth: Penguin, 1970); 'Are Adult Literacy Programmes Neutral?' in Leon Bataille (ed.), *A Turning Point for Literacy* (London: Pergamon, 1975) pp. 195–200.

Gluckman M., 'The Kingdom of the Zulu of South Africa' in M. Fortes and E. Evans-Pritchard, *African Political Systems* (London: Oxford University Press), pp. 23–55.

Gugelberger, Georg M. (ed), *Marxism and African Literature* (London: James Currey, 1985).

Gramsci, Antonio, *The Modern Prince and Other Writings* (New York: International Publishers, 1957).

Halliday, M.A.K., 'Categories of the Theory of Grammar' in *Word 17* (1961), pp.

241–292); *A Course in Spoken English: Intonation* (London: Oxford University Press, 1970); *Language as Social Semiotic* (London: Edward Arnold, 1978); *An Introduction to Functional Grammar* (London: Edward Arnold, 1985).

Halliday, M.A.K. and Hasan, Ruqaiya, *Cohesion in English* (London: Longman 1976).

Heron, George, *The Poetry of Okot p'Bitek* (London: Heinemann, 1976).

Iyasere, Solomon, 'African Oral Tradition – Criticism as Performance: A Ritual' in *African Literature Today* No. 11 (1980), pp. 169–174.

Jacinto, Victor, 'It's No Use' in *Index on Censorship*, Volume 8, No. 1 (1979), p. 31, translated by Nick Caistor.

Jakobson, Roman, 'Grammatical Parallelism and its Russian Facet' in *Language*, Volume 42, No. 2 (1966), pp. 299–429; 'Poetry of Grammar and Grammar of Poetry' in *Lingua* 21 (1968), pp. 597–609.

Jung, Carl Gustav, *The Spirit of Man, Art and Literature* (London: Routledge and Kegan Paul, 1953); *Symbols of Transformation* (London: Routledge and Kegan Paul, 1965).

Kristeva, Julia, *Desire in Language: A Semiotic Approach to Literature and Art* (Oxford: Basil Blackwell, 1980).

Kronenfeld, J.Z. 'The "Communistic" African and the "Individualistic" Westerner' in Bernth Lindfors (ed.), *Critical Perspectives on Nigerian Literature* (Washington D.C.: Three Continents Press, 1979), pp. 237–264).

Kunene, Mazisi, *Emperor Shaka the Great* (London: Heinemann, 1979); 'The Relevance of African Cosmological Systems to African Literature Today' in *African Literature Today*, No. 11 (1980), pp. 190–205; *The Ancestors and the Sacred Mountain* (London: Heinemann, 1982).

Lacan, Jacques, *The Four Fundamental Concepts of Psychoanalysis*, tr. Alan Sheridan, ed. Jacques-Alain Miller (Harmondsworth: Penguin, 1977); *Ecrits*, tr. Alan Sheridan (London: Tavistock Publications, 1977).

Mabala, Richard S. (co-ordinator), *Summons: Poems from Tanzania* (Dar-es-Salaam: Tanzania Publishing House, 1980).

Miroslav, Holub, *Selected Poems* (Harmondsworth: Penguin, 1967).

Mofolo, Thomas, *Chaka* (London: Heinemann, 1981).

Morell, Karen L. (ed.), *In Person: Achebe, Awoonor and Soyinka at the University of Washington* (Seattle: Institute for Comparative and Foreign Area Studies, University of Washington, 1975).

Motlhabi, Mokgethi (ed.) *Essays on Black Theology* (Johannesburg: The Black Theology Project of the University Christian Movement, 1972).

Mzamane, Mbulelo Vizikhungo, *Black Consciousness Poets in South Africa, 1967–1980 with Special Reference to Mongane Serote and Sipho Sepamla* (Unpublished Ph.D. Thesis, University of Sheffield, 1982); 'The Uses of Traditional Oral Forms in Black South African' in Landeg White and Tim Couzens (eds), *Literature and Society in South Africa* (Harlow: Longman, 1984), pp. 147–160.

Neruda, Pablo, *Selected Poems* (Harmondsworth: Penguin, 1975).

Ngugi wa Thiong'o, *Writers in Politics* (London: Heinemann, 1981); *Decolonising the Mind* (London: James Currey, 1986).

Ngugi wa Thiong'o and Ngugi wa Mirii, *I will Marry When I Want* (London: Heinemann, 1980).

Norris, Christopher, *The Deconstructive Turn* (London: Methuen, 1983).

Nwoga, Donatus, 'Obscurity and Commitment in Modern African Poetry' in *African Literature Today* 6 (1974), pp. 26–45.

Ofeimun, Odia, *The Poet Lied* (Harlow: Longman, 1980).

Okafor, R.N.C., 'Politics and Literature in Francophone Africa – the Ivory Coast Experience' in *Okike* No. 23, 1983), pp. 105–130.

Okigbo, Christopher, *Labyrinths* (London: Heinemann, 1971).

Okpewho, Isidore, *The Epic in Africa: Towards a Poetics of Oral Performance* (Columbia University, 1979).

Omer-Cooper, J.D., *Zulu Aftermath* (London: Longman, 1966).

Ong, Walter, *Literacy and Orality* (London: Methuen, 1982).

Pratt, Mary Louise, *Towards a Speech Act Theory of Literary Discourse* (Bloomington: Indiana University Press, 1977).

Royston, Robert (ed.), *Black Poets in South Africa* (London: Heinemann, 1973).

Ryle, Gilbert, *The Concept of Mind* (Harmondsworth: Penguin, 1949).

Sandars, N.K., *The Epic of Gilgamesh* (Harmondsworth: Penguin, 1964).

Sepamla Sipho, *The Soweto I Love* (London: Rex Collings, 1977).

Serote, Mongane Wally, *Selected Poems* (Johannesburg: Ad Donker, 1982).

Sinclair J. McH. and R.M. Coulthard, *Towards an Analysis of Discourse* (London: Oxford University Press, 1973).

Slater, Henry, 'Shaka Zulu, Apartheid, and the Politics of the Liberation of Historiography of South Africa', a paper presented to the Fifth SAUSSC Conference, 1982.

Soyinka, Wole, *Idanre and Other Poems* (New York: Hill and Wang, 1967); 'Neo–Tarzanism' in *Transition*, Volume 48, No. 9 (1974), pp. 54–57; *Myth, Literature and the African World* (London: Oxford University Press, 1976).

Thompson, Leonard, 'Co-operation and Conflict: the Zulu Kingdom and Natal' in Leonard Thompson and Monica Wilson (eds), *The Oxford History of South Africa*, Volume 1 (London: Oxford University Press, 1969), pp. 334–390.

Udoeyop, N.J., *Three Nigerian Poets* (Ibadan: Ibadan University Press, 1973).

Vilakazi, B.M., *Zulu Horizons* (Johannesburg: Witwatersrand University Press, 1973).

Wali, Obi, 'The Dead End of African Literature', *Transition* No. 10 (1963), pp. 13–15.

Wästberg, Per (ed.), *The Writer in Modern Africa* (Stockholm: The Scandinavian Institute of African Studies, 1968).

Williams, Gwyn (ed.), *Welsh Poems: Sixth Century to 1600* (London: Faber, 1973).

Wilson, Monica, 'The Nguni People' in Leonard Thompson and Monica Wilson (eds), *The Oxford History of South Africa*, Volume 1 (London: Oxford University Press, 1969), pp. 76–130.

Wimsatt, W.K., *Versification: Major Language Types* (New York: New York University Press, 1974).

Zingani, Willie T., 'African Mfiti Flight No. 1' in Angus Calder, Jack Mapanje and Cosmo Pieterse (eds), *Summer Fires: New Poetry from Africa* (London: Heinemann, 1983).

Index